Emily Ackerman faced  her
elderly parents. She need d in
vain for a book to help. Sh̲ ̲ d up
writing one herself.

Here is a practical, biblical, truthful, liberating and personal guide to facing one of life's big challenges. I am at the
Chapter 4 stage as a member of the 'sandwich generation',
and found this book offered me hope as well as help.

Ruth Coffey, adjunct tutor, Moorlands College, Christchurch

A super book! Relevant, realistic, faithful to the Bible and
hugely practical, it takes us through the privileges and pains
of caring for elderly parents with an easy-to-read blend
of humour, illustration and profound insight. Impossible
for any carer to read it without being richly helped and
challenged.

Peter Hicks, author of What Could I Say? A Handbook
for Helpers

A Time to Care: Loving Your Elderly Parents is one of the most
touching and challenging books I have read in the last three
years. In a society that praises doing – activism – and neglects
the importance of being, it is refreshing to be reminded that
caring for your elderly parents is not a disturbing waste of
time, but a privilege and an honour that greatly pleases God
(1 Timothy 5:4). Written with sensitivity, a loving heart and
biblical wisdom, I warmly recommend this book as an excellent example of how we can sanctify every situation in life.

Dr Pablo Martinez, psychiatrist and author of A Thorn in
the Flesh: Finding Strength and Hope amid Suffering

A Time to Care: Loving Your Elderly Parents is a timely and warmly written book about the emotional, practical and spiritual aspects of caring for elderly parents. Packed with examples, sound guidance and empathy, it is a must-read for Christians with parents still living.

> *Louise Morse, author of* Could It Be Dementia? Losing Your Mind Doesn't Mean Losing Your Soul

An excellent and practical resource for those caring for elderly parents. Honest, down-to-earth, spiritually sensitive, encouraging and realistic. Filled with helpful suggestions and wise advice drawn from first-hand experience.

> *Professor John Wyatt, Professor of Ethics and Perinatology at University College London, and author of* Matters of Life and Death: Human Dilemmas in the Light of the Christian Faith

A time to care

Dedication
This book is dedicated to my parents, with love and thanks

Emily Ackerman

A time to care

Loving your elderly parents

INTER-VARSITY PRESS
Norton Street, Nottingham NG7 3HR, England
Email: ivp@ivpbooks.com
Website: www.ivpbooks.com

First published 2010

British Library Cataloguing in Publication Data
A catalogue record for this book is available from the British Library.

ISBN: 978-1-84474-487-9

Set in 12/15pt Monotype Dante
Typeset in Great Britain by Servis Filmsetting Ltd, Stockport
Printed and bound in Great Britain by Ashford Colour Press Ltd, Gosport,
Hampshire

*Inter-Varsity Press publishes Christian books that are true to the Bible and that
communicate the gospel, develop discipleship and strengthen the church for its mission
in the world.*

*Inter-Varsity Press is closely linked with the Universities and Colleges Christian
Fellowship, a student movement connecting Christian Unions in universities and
colleges throughout Great Britain, and a member movement of the International
Fellowship of Evangelical Students. Website: www.uccf.org.uk*

CONTENTS

Acknowledgments

I always thought that writing a book would be a lonely task, but not a bit of it. This book, like my life, has a large and interesting cast list.

In the beginning, my parents got old and needed support, and did it all with style and grace. I have not put their personal details into the book out of respect for their privacy, which means that I never got to boast about how cool they really are. My brother and sister-in-law are now doing a tremendous job of caring for them, and this has released me to write this book while things were still fresh in my mind.

I am more than grateful to my carer friends who carved time out of their busy lives to answer lists of personal questions, trusting me to use the answers with respect. Their wisdom and experience have informed every page of this book, far beyond the parts directly quoted. I hope I have made it clear how much I admire each one of them.

Thanks to Revd Humphrey Mildred, Dr Maureen Gowans

and Mrs Cheryl Henderson, who cheerfully took time to give of their expert advice, and to Eleanor Trotter at IVP for being kind, helpful and enthusiastic. Thank you to all the many people whose brains I picked, and those who prayed, listened, read little bits, and generally offered cheerleading services, particularly Gordon, Stephanie, Adele, Sallie and Mo.

Finally, for me this song lyric says it all:

My tongue will be the pen of a ready writer,
And what the Father gives to me I'll sing.
I only want to be His breath;
I only want to glorify my King.[1]

Introduction

We bumped into old friends at a conference and agreed to eat together. As we relaxed after lunch we enjoyed catching up on the news: children, jobs, projects and churches. Presently someone asked, 'So how's your Mum these days?', and we went on to chat about our ageing parents.

I was the youngest there, just beginning on the parent-care journey, and I was squashing down panic. On our return home the following day I knew I would be plunged back into a new and scary world, where my parents' frailty was deepening. I felt isolated, worried and out of my depth.

As we talked, I began to feel that something special was happening to me. I had a sense that here was a place where I could be me, tell the truth, and be understood and loved. It was wonderful to be with people in the same boat, and somehow it all felt strangely familiar.

Finally the penny dropped. I felt as I had done years before, when as young parents we had all huddled together for comfort, deciphering how to raise healthy children in the Christian faith. We had worked as a team, brainstorming, sympathizing, babysitting, cracking black jokes, praying, making crisis phone calls and learning to love one another along the way. The church offered good teaching for parents, and Sunday school for the children. There were good Bible-based books, positive toys and all sorts of resources to help us to parent well. We did the job as a community.

I looked around the room with different eyes. Here was the same possibility, but in another setting. Surely there must be masses of us out there, cooking, praying and keeping company, ringing the GP, trying to track down a shirt like the ones Dad's always worn, and all the rest of it. Where was the support? Where were the equivalents of the toddler groups, the excellent resources on parenting, child development, diet and teenage traumas? Where were the sermons, study groups, Christian books, websites and maga-zines on caring for parents? Didn't we need support, love and encouragement too?

Presently I asked if anyone knew of a good Christian book on caring for parents, to keep me sane when I got back home again. Everybody shook their heads.

'You could write a book I'd like to read,' I said as I looked around at the group. 'I wish someone would write down all the things we've learned so far, for other people in our shoes.' But in the end I wrote the book myself, drawing from the experience and wisdom of many friends, supplying a book that I believe is badly needed today.

A path for real people

I have not been a perfect carer, nor am I as Christlike as I could and should be – just ask my family. All I am qualified to do is to draw you a map of where I've been, writing from painful experience about the many pitfalls that I have landed in, and the strategies that I and others have discovered to dig ourselves out again.

Of course caring for parents is not confined to Christians, and a good thing too! However, my vision is to bring the riches of the Christian faith into the challenges of this task, so there is plenty of Bible teaching in the pages ahead, along with other information, advice and support.

I delved back into the Bible to find God's perspective on parent-caring, with results that surprised me. God has a lot to say about the elderly. The Bible provides inspiring reasons to care for parents, and solid, relevant help and encouragement for carers when the going gets tough. However, since God always looks at the heart, he is also vitally interested in how the process of care might shape a carer's life, so we'll look at that aspect too. We have a lot to gain while going through the season of parent-care.

I've talked to many parent-carers along the way to discover and tackle our big issues: role reversal, stress, embarrassment, time-management, handling a move and dealing with death. I've drawn from my own years of caring for my ageing parents, and what I've learned from the elderly and their families in my work as a doctor. Since I'm now limited physically by chronic illness, I can also give you a peek into how it feels to be in poor health and on the receiving end of care.

This book is designed to be read right through, or dipped into as you need it. Each chapter ends with questions and ideas to ponder or discuss, and quick quotes to take away if you're too pushed for time to sit down and read at any length.

My prayer is that this book will offer you a strong scriptural foundation for the valuable ministry of parent-caring, adding on practical ideas, encouragement and inspiration to give you confidence to serve God effectively.

Dr Emily Ackerman
Edinburgh
April 2010

1. Who, me? Called to care

Many of us tumble into parent-care with no warning, like my brother's spaniel, who danced backwards off the end of the pier in a burst of excitement and found herself unexpectedly wet.

The simple fact is that most people will get involved in some kind of parent-care during their lifetimes. This is often ignored by our society, and sometimes by the church too. If we consider the emphasis on child-rearing, there's a big mismatch, yet more of us have parents than rear children.

Our culture, of course, exerts its own influences, not all of them helpful. We hear a lot about the demographic time-bomb, in other words our ageing population. This very negative term gives us a feeling of panic about caring for the elderly, as if they might explode and kill us all. We make old people into saints ('Isn't she wonderful?') or victims ('Tragic neglected pensioner dies alone'). Either way, they are seen as different from the rest of us, as if they were not quite human.

Meanwhile, arriving at the sharp end of a parental crisis immediately generates difficult emotions and practical problems. We can feel deeply inadequate, embarrassed, sad, worried, sympathetic, yet guilty and resentful . . . and it's only day one. It is difficult to take time out to handle parent-care, and others may not appreciate our absence. We are well out of our comfort zone and looking around for the emergency exit.

We are well out of our comfort zone and looking around for the emergency exit

What is going on? What is God saying to us? Is this emotion-laden task really so important?

God's take on parent-care
God's view of the elderly

To start at the very beginning, the first chapter of Genesis makes it abundantly clear that we are not alone in this life, but related to our environment and to the people around us. We are all carefully created by God in his image, and precious to him. This means that we owe honour and respect to all people, whether young, old, fit and well, or frail and ill.

This is good news for the carer whose parent is weak, agitated, confused, or otherwise very different from the person they used to be. We can continue to respect and honour frail parents because they are made in God's image, and have value and worth to God as individuals. Of course, as 'related' carers we have lifelong memories of the parent when well, which is a solid asset to us in maintaining our love and respect. This too is part of God's amazing strategy to strengthen families and provide loving care for the vulnerable.

Against this background of community life, God gave Ten

Commandments as a basic manifesto for human behaviour. Here is number five:

> Honour your father and your mother, so that you may live long in the land the LORD your God is giving you.
> (Exodus 20:12)

Honouring parents is relevant to children and teenagers still living at home, covering things like not talking back and obeying the household rules. While we live as independent adults, with both generations fit and well, we might find that commandment five takes little effort, but once frail old age sets in, it pops up again big time. Now is the season, our last and best chance, to honour our parents and live out the fifth commandment. Please note, this is not an optional extra for believers. Let's see how Jesus himself handled it.

Jesus expected the Jews to give heartfelt, loving obedience to God while following the Old Testament laws and commandments. The Pharisees preferred to express their religion in endless rituals, living legalistically and without compassion. This cut no ice with Jesus:

> One of them, an expert in the law, tested him with this question: 'Teacher, which is the greatest commandment in the Law?'
> Jesus replied, '"Love the Lord your God with all your heart and with all your soul and with all your mind." This is the first and greatest commandment. And the second is like it: "Love your neighbour as yourself." All the Law and the Prophets hang on these two commandments.'
> (Matthew 22:35–40)

Jesus gives us clear priorities for our lives: love comes first; everything else comes afterwards. Jesus proved his commitment to his words by considering his mother's needs during his own greatest crisis:

> Near the cross of Jesus stood his mother . . . When Jesus saw his mother there, and the disciple whom he loved standing near by, he said to his mother, 'Dear woman, here is your son,' and to the disciple, 'Here is your mother.' From that time on, this disciple took her into his home.
>
> (John 19:25–27)

Here is Jesus dying painfully on the cross. He would not have wasted effort on trivia, so what he did say reflects his top priorities. He assured the dying thief of his eternal destiny, he asked his Father to forgive his enemies and, as we see above, he sorted out care for Mary, his widowed mother. Jesus didn't command the disciple John to take care of her, although this command would no doubt have been obeyed. Instead, he called John to become her loving son. For Jesus, it was truly important that Mary had a son to care for her, someone who would know, respect and love her as well as take care of the practicalities.[1]

Why should I?

Well, all right, God values the elderly and wants them to be well looked after. So what's wrong with leaving it to the experts? Why should it be me?

- I have parents and God expects me to honour them from my heart. This includes taking responsibility for their well-being when they are old. I can't fulfil the fifth commandment without getting involved somehow, although others may be giving day-to-day care.

- I owe them one. Most of us had parents who did their imperfect best to care for us when we were children. Now is a great time to repay them. This response of gratitude is a different thing from the iron shackles of obligation.
- My parents really need me. Hardly anybody gets though old age without needing support at some point, and who better than family tactfully to help someone facing dwindling strength and painful new challenges?
- I know them best. I have an insider track on what they like, hate, enjoy or avoid. This makes for caring that cares, rather than caring that ticks boxes. I see the wider picture because of a lifetime of shared memories, and this too makes for personalized care that is more likely to hit the spot. Nobody wants to be old and frail, and then stripped of their past and judged purely on the basis of today.
- I need to grow. God can use the challenges of parent-care as an opportunity to work on my weaknesses, which might otherwise hide unaddressed.

God's enabling for the task

God has not thrown us in at the deep end and left us to cope alone. Here are two principles to help us rise to the challenge of providing good care for parents.

First, we're not meant to do the job alone. If today finds you exhausted, isolated and crying out for help, please don't throw this book across the room in disgust. We'll be looking at how to build a team in Chapter 3. For now, here's the principle: as believers we are created to work in partnership with God and with others. God intends us to live out his purposes in human community. He also expects his people to walk alongside him, working in close relationship.

Next, God has a long-term plan for each person's life. The need for parent-care may have surprised us, but it didn't surprise him:

> 'For I know the plans I have for you,' declares the LORD, 'plans to prosper you and not to harm you, plans to give you hope and a future.'
> (Jeremiah 29:11)

This lovely promise comes from the book of Jeremiah, a book full of God's loving plans for a disobedient nation. God is full of amazing plans for all of us too. He aims to bless and use each one today, tomorrow and through the rest of life, despite our weaknesses. As part of his lifelong commitment to us, he gives us opportunities to heal, change, grow and learn, so he can use us more powerfully in the future. This is a major fringe benefit to everyone living through the season of parent-care: we can grow and be refined as we cooperate with God. Parent-care brings new challenges into our lives, revealing the secret heart like nothing else, so there is plenty to work on.

Another aspect of this second principle is that God loves us and wants us to live abundantly in every season of life. He has been preparing each carer over the years for this time and this task. It's easy to panic in an unfamiliar situation and forget what we already know to be true. We need to dig deeply and look at applying everything we've got to the task ahead. We have seen that the Bible teaches us to love and care for our parents, so we can serve confidently, sure of God's approval and his provision.

Introducing your instant network

As we focus on caring in community, I'd like you to meet some of my Christian friends who care for parents. I'm very grateful to each one of them for sharing their lives so honestly.[2] Their stories and insights will keep us company throughout the book, and others will be dropping in as well.[3]

Shenaz runs a busy household, with a husband in full-time employment, three children still at home, and older children dropping in, plus her widowed Mum. They started caring for her Mum when she developed early dementia while living alone in another town. Mum moved in with the family while her house was being sold. The plan was to find sheltered housing nearby, but she has now lived with them for eight years.

Mike, who has never married, is the only child of a very elderly widowed mother. They moved in together twenty years ago with an eye to future care. Mike now tries to fit part-time church work around his Mum's growing care needs. Mike has no family support nearby.

Jan, married with older teens and working part-time, has her Mum and her father-in-law Dan to consider. Her Mum lives alone 500 miles away, and is mostly looked after by Jan's sister, Nancy, who herself has major health problems, as well as a special-needs child. Jan visits and phones her Mum and Nancy regularly. Jan and her husband are the only relatives available for Dan, who lives in a nearby care home.

David and his wife are full-time church leaders with a teenage family. David helped his widowed Mum to move into a nearby nursing home when she needed full-time care.

Elisabeth grew up seeing elderly relatives cared for at home. Now she is a wife, mother and grandmother who has been caring for her own parents and aunts for several years. Elisabeth suffered a nervous breakdown due to overload. Since then she has tried to find new ways to balance the demands on her time.

Julie took early retirement because of her health problems. She has never been married. She lives close to her Mum, and took over caring for her when her father died. This has grown into a full-time responsibility over time. Her Mum is now in her nineties and still living alone nearby. Julie's married brothers live and work 100 miles away.

Mhairi and her husband have recently retired, and their children have flown the nest. She oversees her Mum's care in a nearby residential home, the latest twist in a long story of changing needs and care strategies.

What do parent-carers do?

Carers come in different flavours. Some people think that 'caring for a parent' means having them to live permanently in one's home, but this misses the point. Our parents are individuals, with their own histories, wishes, frailties and needs, and so are we. It's no wonder that we care for our parents in different ways.

Mike offers live-in care for his Mum:

> My mother has limited mobility and almost no hearing. To qualify for my carer's allowance I should work thirty-five hours a week. To be truthful, this varies enormously. Direct care – taking her to the toilet, helping her dress, get into bed, etc. – takes a couple of hours a day. Then there's housework, laundry, ironing, cooking and gardening. I'm there to answer the door for any visitors Mum may have (including the doctor and nurse), and when she is able I take her out, both socially and for hospital visits. In addition, I am 'on call' as necessary during the night, which almost makes it 24/7.

Mike's account shows the difficulty of estimating a carer's hours, as time spent supervising and being available

when needed comprises a major unseen part of the
workload.

Jan works effectively to care for two relatives in different
ways, while living with neither:

> I deal with all Dan's legal and financial matters. I visit him and
> buy new clothes for him when necessary. If there are any issues
> to do with his care in the home, I deal with them, also checking
> that medical appointments happen, and chasing up lost results. I
> manage what used to be his flat, getting a tenant when necessary,
> paying all bills, receiving the rent, and then paying it on to the
> home as part of his fees. I encourage my husband to visit Dan
> regularly, and insist that our sons go and see him three times a
> year, and buy and take birthday and Christmas presents for
> him.
>
> Where my mother is concerned, I am at the end of the phone,
> providing a listening ear when she needs to moan, and giving
> advice when asked. Sometimes I go and see her, and stay in her
> home. This involves cooking, shopping, laundry, and escorting
> her to medical appointments. It's a very long round trip, usually
> at no notice.

Carers are very good at downplaying their work. They will
say, 'I don't do much', or 'Anybody would do this', when
actually their work makes a huge difference to a parent's life.
The work of carers also saves the nation massive amounts of
money.[4]

Here is Shenaz's job description. Remember, she looks
after a large family too.

> I prepare all Mum's meals, which means making smooth soup
> because she won't eat anything with lumps in. I give her all her
> medication. I see that she walks a little every day, although she's

not been so keen since she fractured her hip, but she needs the exercise.

I sit with her as long as I can cope with her repetition, make hot drinks during the day, top up the fizzy drink by her chair, and make up her hot-water bottle. I do all her laundry and buy her clothes.

I let in her (state-funded) carers, the doctor, chiropodist, hairdresser and any other visitors. I also have to liaise with the social worker and respite-care organizer. I take her to respite care and name all her clothes, checking she has enough incontinence pads, tablets and fortified drinks with her.

I have to make sure there is always someone around if I am out, in case my Mum needs anything. We have to arrange our life around her, and even when she goes out we have to make sure we're back in time. We can only go out after 8pm because she is put to bed around 7:30 by a carer. I always go and tuck her up and kiss her goodnight.

Shenaz is working flat out and deserves a medal. However, there are many ways to care well for parents, depending on their situation. Here's how David presently attends to his Mum's needs:

I see my mother once a fortnight, alternating between having her to our home and visiting her in her nursing home and taking her out for a meal. We talk on the phone between visits. I was particularly involved with getting her into the home and arranging for the sale of her house and furniture. That was a busy and demanding time, but now things are smooth and straightforward. I wouldn't say that I find any aspect of care hard, except perhaps the emotional drain if my mother is 'down' and weepy.

As we work with frail parents day by day, it may feel as if it's enough to make it to bedtime without a major crisis. We can so easily miss the fact that our actions have a hidden impact on the future. We are living out the spiritual process of sowing and reaping.

Sowing and reaping

I sowed a batch of nasturtium seeds this morning, which was fun. Being an orderly person, I gathered up the compost bag, yoghurt pots, seeds and trowel. I filled all the pots with soil and put them in a tidy row. Once I actually started planting the seeds in the pots, of course, I discovered how hard it is to tell a pot of soil from a pot of soil with a seed hiding in the middle.

Happily, nasturtium seeds germinate in a couple of weeks' time, so I won't have to wait too long to see which pots I missed. However, I will be a bit put out if the seedlings come up as thistles. With seeds, you grow what you sow, and eventually along comes a harvest consisting of more of the same. Unwanted weeds make more weeds, and good plants make more good plants. Each plant produces many seeds, so the yield can multiply dramatically.

Spiritual harvest

This natural process of sowing, growing and then reaping (harvesting) is often used in the Bible to shed light on a spiritual principle. As we live out our lives, our actions and choices are compared to planting seeds, which then grow to affect our own destinies and those of others around us. For example, the prophet Hosea contrasts the good spiritual seeds the people of Israel could have planted with what actually happened: 'Sow for yourselves righteousness, reap the fruit of unfailing love . . . But you have planted wickedness, you have reaped evil, you have eaten the fruit of deception' (Hosea 10:12–13).

If Israel had made better choices as a nation, they would all have enjoyed a harvest of unfailing love. Since they chose instead to plant and tolerate bad seeds in their lives, they found themselves knee-deep in bad consequences.

This is the principle of spiritual sowing: whatever you sow now, you will reap later, with consequences to match. This is easily seen in long-term processes like research, government or child-rearing. After a time of patient effort, the precious harvest starts to appear. Similarly, allowing bad seeds to grow yields painful results.

Another aspect of this principle is that the more seeds you sow, the more you will harvest: 'Remember this: Whoever sows sparingly will also reap sparingly, and whoever sows generously will also reap generously' (2 Corinthians 9:6).

So if as parent-carers we sow seeds of love, patience and perseverance, then the more the merrier. There will be a bigger harvest later. Planting seeds of resentment, hatred or unforgiveness looks like a bad idea, both now and when the seeds grow and multiply.

So where and when will the harvest appear? We can afford to give it some time. Our loving God promises to bless our faithfully sowed seeds of obedience now and over many years to come: 'I, the LORD your God . . . show love to a thousand generations of those who love me and keep my commandments' (Exodus 20:5–6). This promise may seem a bit far-fetched, but read on. Here is a parent-carer in the Bible who sowed good seeds into her difficult situation, with wonderful results.

Ruth, the parent-carer

The short Old Testament book of Ruth tells a gripping story of love, adventure and sacrifice. The young widow Ruth faithfully cared for her depressed mother-in-law Naomi, despite her own bereavement, culture shock and poverty. She showed initiative and persistence, despite loneliness, sadness and the threat of racist attack. Ruth could have lived on in her own country, married again and had her own home and family, but she chose instead to care for Naomi out of love.

Ruth's boss, Boaz, saw and commended her fine qualities:

> I've been told all about what you have done for your
> mother-in-law since the death of your husband – how you left
> your father and mother and your homeland and came to live
> with a people you did not know before. May the LORD repay
> you for what you have done. May you be richly rewarded by the
> LORD, the God of Israel, under whose wings you have come to
> take refuge.
> (Ruth 2:11–12)

The rest of the story dramatically reveals how God placed Ruth and Naomi in a new family and restored their joy again. Looking down through the generations, Ruth's descendants were also chosen for high honour. From her bloodline came King David, and later Jesus Christ himself.[5] The seeds patiently sowed by Ruth grew in her own life and also down the generations into a harvest that changed the world.

God works with each of us as individuals, of course, and will direct our paths and reward us as he chooses. But Ruth's story teaches us the principle of God's favour resting on the faithful carer. The blessing spoken by Boaz also rests on carers today. May the Lord repay *you* for what you have done.

To ponder

1. Are you involved with supporting your elderly parents at present? What sort of things are you doing for them?

2. Did you expect to look after your parents in their old age?

3. Think about what kind of seeds you have sowed into your caring work recently. Are there other seeds you'd like to sow and harvest? Take a little time to pray about the process of spiritual sowing.

'You don't choose your family. They are God's gift to you, as you are to them.' Desmond Tutu

'The elderly need so little, but they need that little so much.' Anon

'A single field poppy flower produces around 17,000 seeds, of which around 3,000 will remain dormant and viable in untilled ground for at least a century before bursting into flower when the ground is disturbed.' Monty Don, gardening expert (from his column in *The Observer*)

'Live a life of love.' Ephesians 5:2

2. But I don't have time: Finding room for caring in your life plan

Parent-caring often comes along when we're in our forties, fifties and beyond, with substantial responsibilities: families to rear, mortgages to pay, responsible jobs or perhaps even a business to run. In church and community life, our age group is often hitting maximum effectiveness. Middle-aged parents may now see family responsibilities easing and start looking to new pursuits. Perhaps we feel comfortable and settled, better off, or full of plans and projects. Any or all of this can be derailed by parent-care responsibilities.

We try to juggle the new with the old, but find we have no time for both. It may be the moment for a more radical rethink of our life plans.

Whose life is it anyway?
Like many other carers, I have felt deeply challenged over my sense of calling. Do I really believe it when I say or sing that my life belongs to God? Does he truly have permission

to send me anywhere he wants to? Have I got a serving heart, or are there limits? 'Oh, but I didn't mean *that!*'

But surely God wants me to serve him?

'Yes, but my ministry, my vocation, my dreams for God's work . . . What about them?' With love and respect I say, the key word in that sentence is 'my'. Ministry is another word for service, and service is all about the one we serve. We can so easily get wrapped up with what *we* want to do, and become deaf to God's prompting to move on with him.

There are two interlinked biblical concepts to get us back on track, back to serving God effectively: a servant-heart attitude and sacrificial living. Although these are not cosy concepts, they bring vision and hope into a season of loss. In hard times I've found it's easier to have a biblical perspective on events, rather than suffering without understanding.

A servant heart

Jesus is our highest example of an individual with a servant heart. Philippians 2:5–9 explains how Jesus laid aside his royal status as the Son of God:

> Your attitude should be the same as that of Christ Jesus:
> Who, being in very nature God, did not consider equality with
>   God something to be grasped,
> but made himself nothing,
>   taking the very nature of a servant.
>   being made in human likeness
> And being found in appearance as a man,
>   he humbled himself
>   and became obedient to death – even death on a cross!
> Therefore God exalted him to the highest place
>   and gave him the name that is above every name.

Jesus, filled with vision and purpose, chose to live a humble life without status or possessions, and spent his time serving the poor. He finally sacrificed his life to save ungrateful humanity. His heart attitude was to serve others at whatever cost to himself. Jesus did not perform acts of service with a secretly superior attitude, but truly from the heart.

He was an effective servant because he was humble enough to be obedient. He did only what his Father told him to do, leaving aside other obvious needs or personal projects. In this way, he completed every act of service he was called to do, although his ministry was only three years long. His life was truly successful, and his Father valued his service highly. The Bible passage tells us to follow his example in assuming a servant attitude and obeying God's call, wherever it takes us.

So caring for vulnerable people made in the image of God is important to him, even if it's not seen as cutting edge. We want to serve God, yet we cannot limit him. We may be called to lay down our previous ministries and activities to make time for God's new call to care for parents, even if others don't understand. Sometimes it takes a long time to believe that God is in our new situation, because we saw his favour so obviously in the last season of life. We cling to the boat, but he is calling us out on to the water.

We cling to the boat, but he is calling us out on to the water

A living sacrifice

Sacrificial living is the visible sign of a servant-heart attitude. The apostle Paul calls us to refocus our lives: 'Therefore, I urge you, brothers, in view of God's mercy, to offer your bodies as living sacrifices, holy and pleasing to God – this is

your spiritual act of worship' (Romans 12:1). Paul teaches
that Christians need to lay down their own lives and personal interests as an offering, rather than worshipping God
through the Jewish tradition of killing animals on an altar.
This is a lifelong struggle for every believer. It's always hard
to let God take control, to surrender our desires and die to
self.

A passage in John 12 helps us to understand how Jesus
found the strength to choose a sacrificial life. Jesus knew
his death was close. His disciples were expecting him to
gain power and throw off the unjust Roman occupation.
They had missed his purpose because they did not understand his heart attitude. Jesus replies with this remarkable
manifesto:

> The hour has come for the Son of Man to be glorified. I tell you
> the truth, unless a grain of wheat falls to the ground and dies, it
> remains only a single seed. But if it dies, it produces many seeds.
> The man who loves his life will lose it, while the man who hates
> his life in this world will keep it for eternal life. Whoever serves
> me must follow me; and where I am, my servant also will be.
> My Father will honour the one who serves me.
> (John 12:23–26)

Jesus links his glorification with his death, which must have
really challenged his listeners. Jesus then explains that, by
dying, he will open the way for a mighty harvest for others.
By 'hating' his earthly life, Jesus is free to lay it down for a
greater purpose. He insists that those who serve him must
follow him, and that the Father will honour these faithful
followers.

Laying down our lives and activities to do as God directs
will be pleasing to him and truly fruitful, although costly.

As we saw in the last chapter, unless we are willing to plant our precious seeds to die in the ground, there can be no harvest.

Real people, real pressures

Elisabeth has been juggling caring work with other parts of her busy life for many years. She used to support her Mum and Dad in their own home. For a while she also oversaw the care of two elderly aunts in another part of the UK. These days she cares for her recently widowed Mum and her remaining aunt, both at a distance and in separate places. Elisabeth's increased caring responsibilities have prevented her from giving more time to 'Christian' work:

> We had hoped that once our children had left home, and we had
> a little more free money, I would be able to join my husband
> on overseas work trips, and that when he retired we would do
> some travelling. We expected to engage more fully in Christian
> missionary work, including some short-term activities overseas.
> This began to happen, but came to a full stop because of caring
> needs and no energy to take on other big projects.

Mhairi's Mum has dementia and has needed more and more care over the years. The intense pressure of Mhairi and her husband's demanding careers, plus overseeing Mhairi's Mum's home-care package, led to big changes.

> I made the decision to leave work ahead of retirement age,
> once financial commitments to our children had lessened. I was
> concerned that, if I could only continue to visit once a fortnight,
> my Mum might very quickly not recognize me as her dementia
> progressed. I wanted to spend more time visiting and less time
> travelling. It was definitely the right thing to do. Our decision to

move house to be nearer my Mum also meant big changes for all the family.

Julie is a single retired woman, so she has no 'excuses' for being away from her beloved but demanding mother, who is agoraphobic, deaf, partially sighted and suffers increasingly from poor memory. Julie tries hard to squeeze in time for sport and voluntary work, as she finds the change of focus very refreshing. Her relationships have suffered due to shortage of time and the effects of stress, leaving her feeling isolated.

Angry with God

Some Christians find themselves struggling privately with difficult feelings about God when their lives are 'disrupted' by parent-care, because they believe that God's providence should protect them from hardship. We can feel disappointed and cheated of our 'rights' when troubles press in, and this makes us feel far from God. 'Doesn't he love us any more?' Satan meanwhile is having fun, 'sympathizing' with us and pointing out that we are very hard done by. What's gone wrong here?

God's promises are sure and permanent, but sometimes we misinterpret them, getting the notion that God's children are guaranteed an easy path, and dwelling on those Bible passages that seem to confirm this idea. There is another side to the overarching scriptural theme of God's protection and provision, making a paradox for us to ponder.

Paul teaches new believers a foundational truth: 'We must go through many hardships to enter the kingdom of God' (Acts 14:22). That's clear enough! Hardships will come to us all in this fallen world, and Christians are not immune. Happily, another great theme of the Bible is that God will not leave us alone in trouble but will watch over us. He promises to comfort us and work with us, to use our troubles for good, to refine and equip us for what lies ahead: 'When you pass through the waters, I will be with you; and when you pass through the rivers, they will not sweep over you. When you walk through the fire, you will not be burned; the flames will not set you ablaze' (Isaiah 43:2).

By accepting God's sure provision for us in every circumstance, and his right to send us through the storm to refine us, we can climb off our wobbly soapbox and enjoy our Father's company again. We can ask God to meet and change us in our circumstances, rather than demanding instant deliverance. This is the path to prosperity – lasting, life-giving spiritual prosperity.

A time of preparation

Sometimes our pain and frustration are simply a matter of timing. We can't see ahead to a new season of life, but God is preparing us for it right now. Rejecting or resenting God's assignment may mean we don't get the training we need.

In Luke 19:12–26 Jesus tells the story of a rich man who left his servants to go away on business. He gave each servant a large sum of money, telling them to put it to work in his absence. When he returned, he asked each man how he had got on. He was pleased with the man who had made the most of his opportunity and promoted him to high responsibility. He also commended the man who had tried his best, but made less, and gave him a promotion that he could handle. The last man, frightened of his master's reaction to failure, had refused even to try: he hid the money so it would not be lost. He got a telling off and lost his chance of promotion.

These three men didn't ask for money to invest: their

employer chose a suitable opportunity to train them and see what they were made of. His interest was in their heart attitudes, revealed in the way they tackled a task they had not chosen nor expected.

God likewise wants to equip and shape us, and he expects us to use our opportunities to the full. We can be sure that our Father knows us through and through. Although our situation may have taken us by surprise, God has good plans in place. His purpose is to stretch his children, not to pull us apart.

Transferable skills

Caring is a demanding season and can leave little or no time for personal development. We can feel stuck in a rut, without opportunities to grow or learn. It's easy to overlook the fact that we are actually learning all sorts of useful things. These are transferable skills, which can be put to use in whatever comes along next. This is a valuable process where the full benefits are often hidden at the time, only to emerge later on.

For example, my son learned to work a stock control system in his job as a sales assistant, and then he moved to another city. Now he's installed a similar system in his new workplace and is training other staff in how to use it.

A skinny teenage shepherd called David learned over time to protect his sheep from predators with a sling and stone. This was just part of his job description. When he found himself suddenly called by God to fight a big thug called Goliath, he had the right skills to add to God's anointing for the job. He had been prepared for his next assignment in the course of his daily life.

Neither David nor my son knew which skill would be

most useful later on, but both worked hard and absorbed whatever was around to learn.

Since the current assignment is caring, let's take the long view for a bit. What transferable skills might a carer acquire to take into the next assignment? A quick brainstorm generated this list. I expect you can think of other things that are specific to your situation.

People skills
- Seeing a different point of view
- Tact and diplomacy
- Handling difficult or stressed people
- Liaison skills
- Advocacy

Technical and practical skills
- Problem-solving
- Organizing
- Handling finance, such as care-home funding, benefit applications, applying for services
- Managing your workload
- Creative thinking
- Research techniques – finding out what you need to know
- Caring skills, such as handling and lifting
- Specific skills to do with your parent's own frailties, such as cooking a diabetic diet, dealing with pain relief, handling memory loss
- Managing stress
- Attention to detail

Character development
- Patience
- Loyalty

- Kindness
- Flexibility
- Compassion
- Perseverance
- Self-control
- Stronger faith
- Personal maturity
- Dealing healthily with personal loss and setback
- Establishing healthy personal boundaries

These are solid, useful things, growing in your life right now. The carer may feel like a field full of weeds, set aside or wasted, but this is not the whole picture. Activities now apparently lying fallow may return enriched later on, or perhaps God has a whole new adventure planned which rests on what you're learning right now.

Elisabeth is aware that God is highlighting problem areas and teaching her as she cares:

> Because caring brings so many situations where I feel helpless, the need to lean heavily on God is very great. In fact when asked how I am, if I don't want to go into detail, I will say honestly, 'Learning!'
>
> I used to think I handed hard things over to God. As I have cared, I have learned that this is *not* the case, and that I carry far too much myself. It has taken a great deal of time and emotional, mental and spiritual focus to keep things going on different fronts. The level of responsibility I carry has been a big challenge . . . This old dog has had to learn new tricks, which is altogether positive.

Transferable skills come easily to those who work with enthusiasm. The same humble job in a fast food café produces one worker who drifts along complaining, and another who works, looks around, learns and moves on up.

'Whatever your hand finds to do, do it with all your might, for in the grave, where you are going, there is neither working nor planning nor knowledge nor wisdom' (Ecclesiastes 9:10). Heartfelt commitment to today's task leads to blessing for the worker who gets more out of his job as he puts more in. The verse continues with a warning that the opportunities of today will not last for ever. God's resources are available to us as we abide in him, and his long-term plan is to bless, refine, train and use us powerfully.

It would be a pity to waste this God-given opportunity to grow.

To ponder

1. Is your life full and busy at present? Looking at your diary, what are your five top priorities in terms of time and energy?

2. Do you feel upset over the pressures and losses you face? Is this harming your relationship with God? Take some time to think and pray over this important issue. Would it help to talk to someone?

3. What do you think about the idea of using parent-caring as a training ground for the future? Have you any other transferable skills to add to the list earlier?

'Courage is grace under pressure.' Ernest Hemingway

'Let us not become weary in doing good, for at the
proper time we will reap a harvest if we do not give up.
Therefore, as we have opportunity, let us do good to all
people, especially to those who belong to the family of
believers.' Galatians 6:9–10

'Life may not be the party we hoped for, but while we're
here we might as well dance.' Anon

3. Some days I want to scream: Dealing with pressure

Did you know that carer stress is now official? Researchers have described 'caregiver's syndrome', affecting a wide range of long-term carers.[1] It's made up of guilt, exhaustion, anxiety and anger, resulting in ill health due to high levels of stress hormones. Burn-out and depression often join the party as time goes on. This is a serious problem affecting many carers, and additionally those in their care.

Parent-care has its own particular triggers for stress:

- It's open-ended, both in time and effort, and tends to get more demanding as time goes on. It's hard to 'budget' your emotions and strength when you don't know how long you will need to keep going, or what will hit you next.
- It comes in middle age, a season with many other significant ties and responsibilities, which forces the carer into daily juggling.

- It's tied up with family dynamics and family history, so it tends to stir up uncomfortable memories or conflicts.
- It can be difficult to balance the wish to respect your ill parent with the need to direct and protect them.
- It's seen by our culture as low status, so there's not much training, workplace provision or financial support available.
- It's often repetitive, and you have to work within the restrictions of your parent's health.
- The problems of old age are not easily fixed, but must be borne over time. The job only ends with the trauma of a parent's death.

These stresses can lead to:

- poor health, both physical and mental
- isolation
- tiredness
- boredom and frustration
- relationship difficulties with your parent or others.

Parent-carers need to find effective ways to tackle stress, or reap the painful consequences. Devoting time to personal needs is not selfish, since a positive, refreshed carer is released to stay healthy and provide good care.

We'll start with God's strategies for handling emotions, and then look at other ways to avoid burn-out.

Dealing with emotions

Carers often struggle with a mixture of difficult feelings day by day.

Shenaz explains:

I feel mostly embarrassment, anger and then guilt. I thought toddlers were embarrassing, but that was nothing compared to teenagers. Oh, how little I knew! Caring for my mother is much worse, probably because she looks as if she should know better. My mother just says it as she sees it.

I felt anger in the beginning of her dementia because she simply didn't remember, even something I'd just said. I felt anger at the number of times I'd have to repeat myself or she repeated herself. Now it's more tiredness and annoyance than anger. Also she doesn't always believe what I tell her, even though it's the truth, because it doesn't suit her!

I feel guilty because I am her carer and surely I shouldn't be having these feelings? It made me think what a horrible person I must be to act in such a way – how could these feelings possibly be in me? But then, we are all sinful.

Then when I help her to undress or dress, I see how frail she is, and I feel protective towards her.

The emotions of fear, sadness, frustration and anger form a natural reaction to loss and uncertainty. This is normal and, to my mind, certainly not sinful. Our chosen response to our emotional reactions is where we sin or follow God. '"In your anger do not sin": Do not let the sun go down while you are still angry, and do not give the devil a foothold' (Ephesians 4:26–27). Paul points out that anger causes trouble when it is given a permanent home, rather than assessed, prayed over and promptly resolved. The anger itself is not a sin or a problem, says Paul, but what happens next might be.

Handling emotions is easier if we understand the way we are made. If we allow emotions to flow in the right channel, they give life, like a clean river flowing along. If we let rip, then that's more of a tsunami, and someone might get very hurt. If we bottle up feelings, on the other hand, they become stagnant and poisoned. Then the next time that anger or frustration surfaces, it's an ulcer. Or chronic negative feelings lurk, waiting to splash all over the next person who happens to cross us. It can feel like holding back a toxic tide, all day, every day.

A tired carer may naturally feel frustration with a fussy, slow-moving parent. He is tempted to act or speak unkindly, but he has a choice: he can act out his feelings on the spot, or resist that path with God's help. Living a life of love is a matter of constant choice. However, those feelings that are held back will need to be resolved; they don't just dissolve in the bath. Since we are built to express or explode, where are unexpressed feelings supposed to go?

Strategies that work

First of all, pray. Here's a direct instruction to tell all:

> Do not be anxious about anything, but in everything, by prayer and petition, with thanksgiving, present your requests to God. And the peace of God, which transcends all understanding, will guard your hearts and your minds in Christ Jesus.
> (Philippians 4:6–7)

Paul wants us to tell God everything, not just the holy bits. It can be difficult to tell messy stuff to God, but look at the psalms of David, and he was a man after God's own heart. Remember, God knows it all already. It's we who need release and the new perspective that we can find only in God's presence. We are called to enjoy a Daddy/child relationship, not stiff religious restraint. Sons and daughters can share freely with a good father, and their father knows that this is a sign of love and trust.

Verse 7 then promises us a deep and lasting peace, so

this strategy of telling God how we really feel has a massive payout. A heart filled with peace is a priceless asset.

Next, reading the Bible can really help to put feelings into perspective, and give encouragement to balance the stress. For example, Psalm 77 describes Asaph's journey from honestly expressed fear and anguish to hope and faith.

Next, get talking. Find a discreet person and talk it out with him or her. If you feel isolated, ask your minister, or try a carers' group, telephone helpline or suitable Internet chat room. (Have a look in the appendix on page 184 for some ideas.) Another family member can provide a safe place to let off steam. This is a good way to support the front line if you are the one a long way off.

Another avenue for venting feelings responsibly is to write them down (or draw them). Try a diary, a letter, whether posted or not, or poetry. It doesn't matter if your efforts are impressive, readable or even polite, so long as they are honest. The point of venting is to take a load off mind and body.

Exercise is a release for the whole person, as well as a health necessity, but time for this can be hard to find. A brisk walk to the shops, a swim or even kicking a cushion will let out some negatives before they spill over in the wrong place.[2]

Some carers have inspirational phrases which they bring to mind at tense moments when they cannot safely walk away, such as: 'Infinite patience', 'It's not his fault' or 'Saved to serve'.

Life in the pressure cooker

Trust in God becomes an urgent matter in the middle of all this. Any fool can trust God when everything is going well. When it comes to turmoil, that's Trust exam time, and the pressure is on: 'The crucible for silver and the furnace for gold, but the LORD tests the heart' (Proverbs 17:3).

Crucibles are hot and the contents can't escape until everything is melted. Then the dross floats to the top for all to see and is skimmed off and thrown away, leaving purer metal behind. The Bible compares God's work in our lives to the refining process. Let's see how this might work out in a caring setting.

A manager, church leader or family head is used to being treated with respect and friendly deference. He works hard, but everything is under control. On the other hand, there is nobody quite like his Mum for cutting him down to size. Suddenly he is out of his comfort zone, with no impressive role or even a lunch break. He is ordered around, emptying bins, making cups of tea and doing other humble tasks. He faces many problems and has no brilliant solutions to offer. He discovers painfully that his caring work is revealing his own hidden weaknesses. God has put him in the crucible.

Still, there's good news, for the contents of the crucible are given this treatment to increase their usefulness and purity, not to destroy them. God values you, even as he turns up the heat. Parent-care is just one setting for God's refining fire, which appears without fail in every believer's life.

Menopausal carers

Another emotional minefield for female carers is the meno-pause. It seems a bit mean really. Just when you need robust health, a calm attitude and all your wits about you, you get mood swings, hot flushes, insomnia and all the rest. This issue can seriously affect a carer's emotional and physical well-being, and ignoring it will not make it go away.

Medical advice is helpful, and you may need to persevere with trying out various approaches, despite lack of time for yourself. There are different types and dosages of medications and supplements, and it's common for women to have a few trial runs before settling on the best solution.

Explaining what is going on to your household, if you live with others, may ease relationships. Even a child can understand that Mum is feeling extra tired, grumpy, hot or whatever. Teenagers can be told that Mum too has hormonal mood swings. Your own Mum, meanwhile, has been through it herself and might have some good advice. Or perhaps you'd rather keep your health private from the family and discuss it only with your doctor or a close friend.

Telling the truth

Unrealistic expectations pile on the pressure and rob carers of peace and satisfaction at work. Here are some truths about caring. How do they strike you?

- God never promised us a trouble-free life.
- Caring is hard work and not always enjoyable.
- We are not invincible and untiring, but need rest and fun.
- We will never behave perfectly this side of heaven.
- We are likely to have times of illness, distraction or low mood. At such times we will not be able to run a normal level of service.
- Worrying doesn't achieve anything.
- We don't have to do everything ourselves in order to be good carers.

On that final point, sharing the care without guilt is really important for stress management, so let's explore it now.

Sharing the care
The moment of truth

I'd like to print the following paragraph in neon yellow if I could, because it's so important!

Many carers hit a day when they are no longer able to fill the growing gap between Dad's abilities and his daily needs. This is a natural consequence of age-related decline, so there's not much point going on a guilt trip, even if Dad thinks otherwise.

Every family is different, so every parent-care situation is unique. The common factor for us all, however, is this: frail parents get more needy over time, and their carers get more tired. In the light of this, sharing the care is not failing to care. It makes sense to respond to decline promptly by seeking help, rather than sticking your head in the sand. Unrealistic or outdated caring can push you or your parent into depression or other avoidable illness or mishap. Your job as a carer is to ensure that your parent's needs are met, not to do everything by yourself.

> *Sharing the care is not failing to care*

Superman Syndrome

As a child I loved cartoon superheroes, like Superman. Remember Batman, with his faithful sidekick, Robin? It may seem easier to care single-handedly, like Superman, relying on nobody else, but this is not God's best for the carer or the parent. We need to be like Batman and learn that teamwork is super cool.

Carers often feel they are left to do it all by themselves, but we may be missing something. Out there, paid for with our tax contributions, are paid professionals whose job it is to make life easier for all of us. There are doctors who can advise about health issues, nurses to teach the practicalities, social workers to help us find what's available locally, and benefit uptake officers to show which benefits we can claim. There are voluntary organizations dealing with the elderly, and groups focusing on a particular illness or health problem. There are people running clinics, day hospitals, lunch clubs, assessment centres and respite homes. All these people are there to help, but you need to ask them. They can't just read your mind, can they?

Then there are the friends who say, 'If there's anything I can do . . .', to which we smile sweetly, say 'thank you', and never ring them back. After all, they didn't really mean it, did they?

Letting God in

Another form of Superman Syndrome affects the Christian carer. Grasping God's priority on parent-care, we valiantly try to do it all by ourselves. This ignores God's pattern of commissioning: he always gives a task to do in partnership with him. For example, here is the way Jesus sent out his disciples after his resurrection: 'Again Jesus said, "Peace be with you! As the Father has sent me, I am sending you." And with that he breathed on them and said, "Receive the Holy Spirit"' (John 20:21–22). The promise of God's Spirit is not a minor bonus; it is the path they are commanded to follow. God does not just send people out, he leads them out.

'I am the vine; you are the branches. If a man remains in me and I in him, he will bear much fruit; apart from me you can do nothing' (John 15:5). This verse contains a useful principle for carers. It may feel easier some days just to DIY, but God's way, as always, bears fruit. We want to see good results from our caring work, but we can end up missing out when we work alone. Doing God's work in God's way with

God's resources makes for the best possible result. Imagine your own family blessed by the fruit of the Spirit growing in you: love, joy, peace, patience, goodness, kindness, faithfulness, gentleness and self-control (Galatians 5:22–23).

Building a team

OK, here we are, working in partnership with God and ready to delegate. So where are those willing helpers?

It feels like a lot of extra effort to look, or ask, for help, but then you know already how much you stand to benefit. Tracking down services, filling in forms and chasing up professionals can feel intimidating at first. But if you can see this as part of caring for your parent *properly*, perhaps it will get better. This approach also helps with other aspects of caring work that you don't like. Experience shows that any job or occupation has less pleasant aspects in the mix.

Team building works like a treasure hunt. First think about what kind of help you need (respite care, hot meals, a regular visitor, a stair lift?) and go hunting for it. You will probably find other treasures along the way, which you might use now or keep for later on. Other carers, the phone book, the library, your local council website, your doctor and voluntary organizations such as Help the Aged are all good sources of advice on where to look for what you need. If someone can't help you, ask them if they know someone who can.

Back to the forms . . . Carers are doing a fantastic job of making vulnerable people comfortable and happy, and the government should be falling over itself to help. If it isn't, maybe it needs a reminder from you. You might be able to claim benefits or free services for yourself or your parent that would make all the difference day by day.

If you care for someone for a substantial amount of time

on a regular basis, whether you live in or not, you are legally entitled to request a carer's assessment from social services. This is a great opportunity to ask for what you need to keep the show on the road.

Supervising carers and services from different agencies can be surprisingly time- and energy-consuming. Still, getting on top of this aspect will contribute to the parent's quality of life, as well as giving some breathing space to the carer in the longer term.

Handling offers of help

It may seem awkward to follow up on friends who offer help, or to ask for help, but think how you would feel if you offered help to a friend and they never followed it through. Chances are you really meant your offer, and chances are so too do they. Likewise, you would want to know if your friend or a fellow church member was struggling and you were in a position to give a bit of help, wouldn't you?

Here's a useful tip for when friends offer to help. Smile and reply, 'Thank you, that's very kind of you. Can I add your phone number to my list of people who've offered help, and ring you later with a couple of specific ideas? No pressure if it doesn't suit.' This lets the person know that their offer is welcome, but that they will not be expected to take on too much. I have found that people respond well to this approach, often offering again after doing their bit, and it's very comforting to have a little list of helpers.

Even the most self-sufficient carer may catch the flu, and will need a holiday. In fact, every care-giver is also in need of care and support. Organizing a bit of wiggle room now could save the day later on.

The assertive carer

If the extended family is not rallying round, they may just be feeling scared of being swamped, or not know what to do. They may worry about offending you or a parent by offering unsuitable help, and remember they can't read your mind. Speaking up and asking someone to do a particular errand or task can make a way for them to get involved. A sibling could be asked to take over for a specific weekend or afternoon so that you can have a break, which will also have the benefit of showing them how things really stand with Mum. Being the one who does the most does not elect you to do everything, and she's *their* Mum too. Don't deny others the blessings sown by carers.

Of course, some carers may have few (or no) family members available to help or advise. These carers will need to lean more heavily on friends and statutory services. Isolation erodes good care.

Adapt and survive

Parent-care can be hectic, and your chosen ways of relaxing – such as hobbies, sport or friendships – may get squeezed out just when you need them most. The trick here is to get creative and see how your pastimes could be adapted. It will not be exactly the same as before, but you can often find new and satisfying ways to connect with previous activities.

Shenaz is particularly good at this:

> I garden in all weathers and I like to pray while I garden. We have a baby alarm which I take into the garden in case my mother shouts out. I am currently trying to finish writing some children's stories and illustrating them. I sit by Mum's bed sometimes with a notepad on my knees.

Time off is a vital element in a carer's life. Making space for this might take a lot of planning, but it allows for a happier, more balanced life. It is not selfish to plan for respite 'just' to allow yourself to enjoy some personal room or to use your time off strictly for your own pursuits.

If it's currently impossible to enjoy long periods relaxing with friends, how about short phone chats, emails or brief visits? Emails or letters are particularly undemanding, as they can wait till you have time to enjoy them.

Day off lite

It can be really hard to find time off, but if a proper weekly day off is not possible at present, then here's a nifty trick I discovered when I had two tiny children: the 'day off lite'. Choose any day of the week and do some planning. On that day, only do what that day demands, leaving all non-essential jobs for the next day. Choose the easiest possible options for cooking, caring or dealing with others and, if you get a break, use it for yourself, not to catch up on more jobs. The change of pace may not be all that startling, but a change of attitude is restful.

I need help NOW!

Sometimes it all gets too much, even for the most devoted and well-organized carer. If you are not coping and fear you may snap and hurt your parent or yourself, a frank phone call to a doctor brings prompt attention and usually an emergency short-term residential placement for the person you care for. Asking for help urgently does not make you a bad person, nor are you the only one in this position. This level of stress you're facing is a clear sign that it's time to reassess your workload.

Who's the boss?

In Matthew 25:31–46, Jesus tells the story of God's judgment day. Those who serve the vulnerable are praised. In fact, Jesus says that whatever we do to serve the least of humanity, we do for him. Yes, cries the harassed carer with awkward parents, but Jesus would be so much easier to serve! However, Jesus is not talking about nice people, but the weak and needy, 'the least of these brothers of mine'. This is an unavoidable call to serve the unlovely.

I see another key truth for carers here. We are called to have a heart attitude of serving *Jesus*, not to run round in circles frantically meeting the claims of others. We are called to be Jesus' hands and feet, so we can serve like him, confident in the face of many needs and expectations. If we have done what he asks, we have done enough, even if the person in front of us is not satisfied. Jesus is present each day as our manager, and we can look to him for validation.

This principle of connecting daily work with God is also seen in this prayer, written by the great leader Moses:

> May the favour of the Lord our God rest upon us; establish the work of our hands for us – yes, establish the work of our hands.
> (Psalm 90:17)

So we can pray that God will lift our all-too-human care work on to a sound and permanent footing. This verse holds another secret: the word 'favour' could also be translated 'beauty'.

May the beauty of the Lord rest upon us as we offer our work to him, transforming the mundane into something extra special.

To ponder

1. Are you stressed by your caring efforts? How does this affect you?

2. What are your feelings and reactions as a parent-carer? Write a list. Pause for private prayer and tell God about each item on your list.

3. What do you think about Superman Syndrome? Are you working towards sharing the care with others? How about leaning on God day by day?

4. Have you had to give up hobbies, work or friendships to make time for parent-care? Is there any way you could adapt these to fit into your current lifestyle?

5. Do you think it's time to change your parent's support set-up to reflect current needs?

'There's never enough time to do all the nothing you want.'
   Bill Watterson
'There are some things you learn best in calm, and some in
   storm.' Willa Cather
'Come to me, all you who are weary and burdened, and I
   will give you rest.' Matthew 11:28
'I try to take one day at a time, but sometimes several days
   attack me at once.' Jennifer Yane
'If you won't feel it, he can't heal it.' Anon

4. The sandwich generation: Extended family caring

The sandwich generation is a term coined to describe those with responsibilities for children below and parents or grand-parents above. Grandchildren, dogs, careers and DIY also make it into the recipe. As a life season, it's stressful, busy and full of opportunities.

If I have to be a sandwich, then I'd like to be a fat, satisfying one, with loads of stuff falling out at the edges. However, as one hard-pressed single dad-cum-parent-carer painfully remarked, 'What's in the middle? Chopped meat!' We may feel stretched far too thinly for the amount of bread, or squashed flat by the pressure of both sides. There is no room for extra crises, but somehow they come up all the time.

So, are there any good points to the sandwich way of life? A cast of thousands is confusing and stretching, but on the other hand *someone* is bound to make us smile some time soon. Also, try as we might, we haven't time to obsess over any one person's problems for too long before the next thing happens.

Time to share

As we have seen, God's best for us involves community living, sharing the ups and downs of life with him and with other people. For the caring extended family, this means rotas, allocated tasks and other forms of delegation. Even a young child can benefit from taking on a household task, if he is shown how to do it properly, and the results are praised and appreciated regularly.

Of course, children need time for play (and homework) and should not be burdened with too much too soon, but my son and daughter grew up with a sick Mum and learned very early on to help me tidy up and do other simple chores. They were trained to handle adult jobs, but we still treated them like beloved children. They really took a pride in their work, and now as adults they are expert in household matters, a blessing to them and to their housemates.

Many recently married couples argue hurtfully over who does the chores. The root of this problem is that one or both partners have no experience of household routines. I believe that part of a parent's responsibility towards a daughter or son is to train them over the years in cooking, cleaning, budgeting, laundry and shopping, for their future happiness and health. Their future spouse will in time be grateful for it, too. 'He who spares the rod hates his son, but he who loves him is careful to discipline him' (Proverbs 13:24).

Even if parent-care forces you to involve your offspring in the work of the household, you are still doing them a favour. The children may not appreciate this at the time, but parents have a God-given mandate to take a lead in the home. It's another part of carefully rearing the family, like the father in

Proverbs, even if it seems quicker and easier to do everything yourself and avoid the hassle.

It's harder if your children are teens and have never lifted a finger, but linking jobs to allowance soon gets good results, after the initial outrage, and they truly need the training before leaving home. If an elderly parent lives in, is there any job they could take on? They probably dread being useless. Also, Mum (or Dad) the Martyr is no fun to be around. Everybody stands to gain from sharing the work.

Blessing the family with parent-care
It's good to live out a biblical lifestyle for our children to see, and that includes caring for the elderly. The trouble starts when we become too busy to give our children or grand-children (or spouse) all the attention they need. This clash between parent-caring responsibilities and other important priorities is where the stress really kicks in. However, the great thing about family life is that there is usually time to make amends and rebalance the mix. Today may not be well balanced, but how about the rest of the month, or the whole year?

A sandwich carer's work involves fostering health, dignity, growth and empowerment among family members, and that includes the carer. We may feel that our own lives and hopes are set aside while we serve and empower others, but, as we saw in Chapter 2, we are learning and growing in ways we may not see at present.

If you are caring for a parent-in-law, by honouring them you are honouring your spouse. I treasure and appreci-ate every act of loving service that my husband gives my parents, on its own merits and as an act of love to me too.

Jan has found unexpected benefits from caring for two elderly relatives:

As my husband and I each have one parent left who demands attention, there's been a new working together as a team, just as if they were the kids, and the understanding between us has been good. It's taught our kids the reality of old age and how to relate to their grandparents respectfully, helping them see that their grandparents' understanding is limited, and how to talk to them appropriately, but also being able to laugh with us later. All my grandparents were dead by the time I was five, so this is teaching them what I never knew. We are also modelling how to relate to elderly parents, but I still hope for a higher standard from my kids towards us when the time comes!

Nuclear family or nuclear meltdown?

Western culture makes an idol out of the 'happy family': Mum, Dad and two matching children. This nuclear family is a modern Western idea. In much of the world, family means a much bigger group, including grannies and grandads, aunties, cousins, and even a black sheep or two for good measure.

Our whole community suffers from the expectation that 'me and mine' must come above all else, including the well-being of other relatives. There is a modern saying: 'Friends are the new family', which takes it a step further, and lets us off all the inconvenient family stuff.

In fact it takes away the pressure to aim at a happy extended family rather than a perfectly run nuclear one. In a larger group it is unlikely that every member will be happy at any given time; so the stakes are lower, and those feeling fine today can support those who are feeling fed up.

Sandwich carers are forced to focus and get creative in spending special times with different family members, which may be an advantage. 'Short and sweet' is the motto that comes to mind for this life season, in marriage, elder-care

and parenting too. This approach also applies to time off.
Ten minutes locked in the loo with the newspaper can work
wonders.

Parent-care is a season, like having the place full of noisy
teens, the confusion of moving house, or dealing with a
sleepless baby. It is not a life sentence, since whatever is happening right now, good, bad or mixed, will surely pass.

Here's Elisabeth, reflecting on the pressures within her
extended family:[1]

> My husband has had to manage with much less support and
> attention from me and, when I was ill, he took over my role
> supporting my parents for a while. He also took early retirement,
> partly so that he could help me with my parents. The way we tick
> as a couple has had to change a great deal to take into account my
> parents' needs.
>
> One of the things that my husband finds difficult is the fact
> that my parents have been so dependent on me that, when he
> and I are both visiting them, he struggles to find a meaningful
> role. We're working on it! But I find his support comforting and
> invaluable.
>
> We have three children and five grandchildren. We lost a
> grandchild early in our time of parent-caring. I'm sure that all our
> children would have wanted us to be more directly involved in
> their lives, particularly in support of the grandchildren. Balancing
> out all the needs is a challenge, and I'm sure we haven't always
> got it right.

Who's looking after whom?

You may feel that your frail parents are unsuitable companions for your children, and of course it's not good to
give children too much caring responsibility. A minority of
children miss school regularly in order to look after elderly

relatives. This is both unfair and against the law. On another front, Granny's idea of suitable child or teen behaviour may not coincide with yours, which is confusing for the children. Mum or Dad may end up as referee on top of all the rest of it. A live-in grandparent needs and deserves to have discipline strategies, and their part in them, clearly explained.

Children often accept disability very well. Sometimes they can break into the world of a sick old person in ways that you can't, while at other times they will need rescuing. Teenage moods plus an unpredictable old person may not be a good mix, or then again they might all cheer up and start ganging up on the parents. The sandwich carer can feel like a teacher on a school outing, smile firmly fixed as she jollies the group along, eyes constantly swivelling for signs of trouble.

Even in a loving family, nobody is responsible for another person's happiness. We all must respond to life's ups and downs as well as we can, and that includes crabby children, moody teens, fussy grannies and even a barking dog.

Please listen to me

'Nobody has time to listen any more,' is a common refrain from the elderly, and they might well be right. As their carer, you may be rushing to get everything done, and finding it difficult just to sit and listen. It can feel like a boring waste of time, especially if you've heard those tired old stories many times before. Dementia adds endless repetition to the mix as a sad reminder of decline.

What is the point of listening? Does it make any difference to the speaker? I believe it does. First of all, listening meets the heart cry of the suffering one. Job cries out to his long-winded friends in frustration: 'Listen carefully to my words; let this be the consolation that you give me' (Job 21:2). Job, like the rest of us, knows what he needs in hard times. We all long to tell our story, to be noticed, valued and significant.

The act of listening affirms that the speaker is important to the listener, more important than anybody or anything else in the world during that time. Your frail parent is living through challenging times, and may really appreciate a chance to talk things through. Even if you can't change or solve anything, your listening presence is a true support.

And there's another factor here. The book of Proverbs was written as a gift and guide from King Solomon to his son. Here is Solomon's comment on wisdom: 'Wisdom is supreme; therefore get wisdom. Though it cost you all you have, get understanding . . . Listen, my son, accept what I say, and the years of your life will be many. I guide you in the way of wisdom and lead you along straight paths' (Proverbs 4:7, 10–11).

God gave us parents to teach us from their wisdom and experience, yet over time we can become disrespectful of our own parents and cease to attend to them. Maybe your parent still has some things to teach you, whether offering a good example or an awful warning.

Not AGAIN

So what about those cheesy family stories, or the familiar list of woes? Perhaps an old person, who rarely gets out and about, has no new topics to discuss. The stories may bring back times when they felt they had more to offer. Telling the story and having it heard brings pleasure and comfort to the teller, and surely that is the point. You don't need to be entertained or informed for listening to make a difference. The subject matter is not as important as the interaction, although sadly this does not make stale old stories any more appealing.

Yet active listening can involve insightful questions to bring fresh understanding to the speaker. If a gloomy old person is given the chance to explore their troubles in more depth, they may find their own solutions, or a more positive approach to the insoluble, failing which, distraction might do the trick.

Perhaps listening time could become a chance to sit down for a minute with a cup of tea, or even to catch up with sewing on buttons, preparing vegetables, ironing or other tasks. It's much easier to listen calmly with something else to do. However, Dad needs to know that he has your attention, even if your hands are busy.

A small child – if you have one to hand – does love a story, and if it's a familiar story, so much the better. Both Granny and child can enjoy storytime together, particularly if a photo album is involved, and the slow pace that frustrates a busy adult is no problem to the child. A teenager might be persuaded to borrow a camcorder and record a grandparent's stories, perhaps focusing on their childhood or wartime memories. This prompts new thoughts and memories for the old person to ponder, and will act as a keepsake for future generations, too.

An old person might appreciate encouragement to write down their memories for posterity. There are special journals now available[2] or they can just note down any thoughts that come to mind. For those with memory loss, a scrapbook, photo album or memory box (with notes and captions as memory prompts) give satisfaction, aid conversation and anchor them in their world.

Where did I put my Bible anyway?

The milk's run out, the cat has just had kittens in the wardrobe, and Mum is icing a birthday cake at midnight. Time for

The milk's run out, the cat has just had kittens in the wardrobe, and Mum is icing a birthday cake at midnight. Time for God is hard to find

God is hard to find. Since God wants us to do the tasks he gives us in his strength, we need to find new ways of receiving from him in order to manage new feats. One of the biblical titles of the Holy Spirit is 'Paraclete', the one who comes alongside to carry the other side of your load. God is comfortable right in the middle of your busiest day, unflustered and full of strength and joy. How can we tune into this wonderful presence?

Brother Lawrence wrote his famous book *The Practice of the Presence of God*[3] while working in a monastery kitchen, a job he cheerfully admits he wasn't very good at. However, he was very good at including God in the daily tasks. Here's a snippet from him: 'It is a great delusion to think our times of prayer ought to differ from other times. We are as strictly obliged to cleave to God by action in the time of action as by prayer in the season of prayer.' His aim was to meet God in the mundane or stressful tasks of the day, rather than being drained until he must stop working to return to God for a refill.

The idea is to feed like a deer, who grazes for most of its waking hours, rather than like a python, who fasts for a month, eats the deer in one gulp and then takes a week-long siesta while the food settles. (Yes, I wish you could have a week-long siesta too!)

God's endless resources

On the last and greatest day of the Feast, Jesus stood and said in a loud voice, 'If anyone is thirsty, let him come to me and drink.

Whoever believes in me, as the Scripture has said, streams of living water will flow from within him.' By this he meant the Spirit.

(John 7:37–39a)

Jesus explains here that we're supposed to be filled to over-flowing with the Spirit of God, rather than running on empty. Since we know that parent-care is at the centre of God's purpose and will, we can ask with confidence to be filled to the brim as we whiz through our days. The gracious hand of God is upon us as we serve. It doesn't matter if our tasks are humble and our status low. If we are serving faithfully, con-nected to God, this opens up the way for a miracle.

The well-connected carer
Carers can start small and grow over time, learning to live so that we are constantly connected to, and nourished by, God's presence. In this way we can bring the flavour of God with us wherever we go. Here are some easy ideas to try.

- Use an audio version of the Bible to bless you as you travel or work.
- Stick a helpful Scripture or prayer to the dashboard, kitchen cupboard or loo mirror, so that it catches your eye throughout the day.
- Play suitable music as you go. Use your own CDs, try Christian radio, or sing, in or out of tune. Positive music is calming and creates a sense of worship and peace.
- Use phrases to welcome God along the way, such as 'God is here', 'Thank you, God', 'This is holy ground' or 'Help, God!' You can speak aloud or just think about the phrase.
- Offer up your work to God as worship day by day.

- Use time in the shower or bath to pray for cleansing and
  forgiveness, time eating or drinking to ask for spiritual
  nourishment, and so on. These triggers to prayer will
  become automatic over time.
- Charismatic readers can use the gift of tongues, silently
  or aloud as appropriate.
- Pray silently for your parent as you give out pills. God
  can bless their medication to their body, as we pray
  when saying grace over food.

Here's how Mhairi's spiritual life changed because of
caring:

> For a while, when every waking minute of life seemed to be
> filled with family, work and dealing with my mother, things like
> regular 'quiet times' just didn't happen. Praying on the hoof was
> more the pattern. However, in extreme moments, either a useful
> scripture came to mind, or someone phoned just when it helped
> to speak.
>
> More often than not I was too exhausted to make it to church.
> The services that I did attend did not seem to speak into what I
> was facing at the time. It was more the fellowship of love, prayer
> and Bible study shared in the house group that helped to sustain
> me through the most difficult phases.
>
> During all my journeying, listening to the radio was a great
> help, as was listening to Christian teaching tapes to restore my
> equilibrium after stressful visits.

The wonderful benefits of learning to live in God's presence
will last far beyond the season of parent-care, of course.
Indeed, you could look on them as a lifelong preparation for
heaven.

To ponder

1. Are you a sandwich carer? How's it going?

2. Would you agree that giving children or teens appropriate household responsibilities is part of a parent's remit? What are your strategies for sharing out the chores when time is tight?

3. Do you think that spending time listening is useful? How do you think your parent views these times?

4. Are you a python or a deer? Are your usual ways of connecting with God working well in your present season of life?

'Been taken for granted? Imagine how God feels.' Anon
'Being pretty on the inside means you don't hit your brother and you eat all your peas – that's what my grandma taught me.' Lord Chesterfield
'The hurrier I go, the behinder I get.' Dutch proverb
'Youth looks forward, old age looks backward, and middle age looks worried.' Kent Crockett
'We ought not to grow tired of doing little things for the love of God, who regards not the greatness of the work, but the love with which it is performed.' Brother Lawrence
'Cast all your anxiety upon him because he cares for you.' 1 Peter 5:7

5. Cutting the apron strings: Being a grown-up around your parents

Many families are taken aback when their settled relationships change in the caring years. Suddenly there are new issues such as enforced intimacy, boundary and privacy problems, role reversal and loss, laid over the original features of this lifelong family bond.

Role reversal is triggered when the parents who used to house, nurture, supervise and lead the family are now in need of some or all of these functions themselves. Then again, some children never received proper care from their parents, yet are trying to look after them now.

Parents and carers face major, uncomfortable life changes imposed on them by new limits, responsibilities and difficulties. These same difficulties may also directly change a parent's outlook or behaviour, and so affect relationships.

Losing independence, well-being and a former way of life is a very hard thing to do gracefully, and your Mum or Dad may not manage it straightaway, if at all. Meanwhile, you are watching the changes in your parent and seeing what they may mean for you. It's no wonder that tempers fray. This is a painful transition for all concerned.

In the face of these big issues, we need to redefine ourselves as individuals, carers and family members, so that we can do our work well. Whether or not our parents are able to rise to the challenge of change, we can learn to respond maturely.

Seeing clearly who I am

So how are we to find solid ground in a changing family? A useful passage in James 1 explains that Christians are meant to be formed and informed by obeying God's Word:

> Do not merely listen to the word, and so deceive yourselves. Do what it says. Anyone who listens to the word but does not do what it says is like a man who looks at his face in a mirror and after looking at himself, goes away and immediately forgets what he looks like. But the man who looks intently into the perfect law that gives freedom, and continues to do this, not forgetting what he has heard, but doing it – he will be blessed in what he does.
> (James 1:22–25)

Our self-image (and hence behaviour) is to be lovingly shaped by God. He uses his powerful Word to reflect the truth about us, whether or not that truth flatters and pleases us. As we read and obey the Word, we learn more about our true selves, and so are able to tackle weakness and grow to be more like him.

This brings us healing, strength and maturity, but basing our self-image on the ideas of those around is like using a distorted mirror. We will never see the whole truth about ourselves from our own notions or memories, or from people we know, no matter how close they may be.

This process of finding true identity doesn't happen automatically, particularly in a world where we are bombarded with other ways of looking at ourselves. We need to take action, to come often into God's presence, to refresh our understanding of God's love for us, and to assess constantly popular images of success, beauty or wisdom in the light of the Word.

New life, new clothes

In Colossians 3:1-9 Paul instructs the Colossians to change their old ways of thinking and behaving, because as Christian believers they have already been changed inside. Paul then moves on to the next step: '. . . and [you] have put on the new self, which is being renewed in knowledge in the image of its Creator' (Colossians 3:10). Paul's choice of words suggests changing old clothes for new. He is telling the Colossians to change their visible behaviour, to reflect the unseen work of God transforming their hearts. Next, Paul defines these new clothes: 'Therefore, as God's chosen people, holy and dearly loved, clothe yourself with compassion, kindness, humility, gentleness and patience' (Colossians 3:12).

The starting point in verse 12 is our place in God's love and purposes. Paul uses the traditional words included in an Old Testament covenant: 'chosen, holy and dearly loved', to highlight the truth that we are in a permanent New-Covenant relationship with God through Christ. Our place as believers is eternally secure. Our motivation for change then flows from this secure identity. We can serve, resting in God's love, rather than striving to earn his love through our service.

Once that foundation is in place, Paul tells us to choose

to put on clothes from a wardrobe of compassion, kindness, humility, gentleness and patience. Now there's a classy
outfit for any carer! This passage teaches that a changed
understanding of self leads on to changed behaviour. The
exciting truth is that it works both ways. Behaviour comes
around to affect self-image and the image we project to
others.

So here are two interlocking scriptural principles:

1. God's Word is given to teach us who we are.
2. God's Word is given to teach us how to live and act.

These two principles work together when we choose to
cooperate with God. Now add God's powerful purpose to
make us more like him, and we're really on to something.
We can tap into an upward spiral that changes the way we
feel and behave, even during difficult times. This frees us to
make healthy life choices in the light of God's Word, regardless of others' choices or attitudes.

To grow in this area, we need to understand where to
draw the line between ourselves and other people.

God-given boundaries

A significant part of spiritual and personal growth is defin-
ing suitable limits around a person's life – setting personal
boundaries.[1] Briefly, personal boundaries are instinctively set
by individuals to protect themselves from unwanted intru-
sion or damage. We were created to live as separate beings
and to see that others also are separate.

The Ten Commandments teach us a lot about how to
maintain healthy personal boundaries. God first commands
us in Exodus 20:1–12 to take responsibility for what's on
our side of the fence. This means loving God, respecting his

name and his Sabbath, avoiding idolatry, loving others and honouring parents. We are not commanded, or able, to take responsibility for another adult's inner life, such as loving God for them: that is their job.

Next, in verses 13–17 we are commanded to respect the property, relationships and personal boundaries of others. This means avoiding offences against another: taking some- one's life, stealing their property, running off with their spouse, telling lies in court to gain selfish advantage over them, and coveting their belongings. God teaches us to set clear limits, what's mine and what's his, for everyone's benefit.

Most difficulties between people come down to boundary disputes. Even if the other person has a poor idea of what constitutes suitable boundaries, if your own boundaries are secure, you are in a stronger position with them. This is not the same as being unloving or selfish. We are only respon- sible for our 'property' – what lies within our own boundar- ies – and we cannot own or control another person. We are responsible before God *to* others, to love, serve and respect them, but not responsible *for* others, taking on their lives and problems as if they were our very own.

What about sacrificial living and the servant heart, though? Where does that fit in? As we saw in Chapter 2, looking at Philippians 2:5–9, Jesus pursued his own heavenly agenda, rather than being yanked around by the demands of others. His choice to serve the poor was based on his knowledge of his own royal identity. His secure boundaries released him to reach out and care deeply for others, and finally to lay down his life.

Parent-carers have a specific boundary issue to handle, which relates to the past. Coming back into relationships originally formed in childhood, we need to find a way in which to redraw the boundaries so that we have a sound basis for our work and well-being. Meanwhile, the frail parent is also forced to deal with changing personal boundaries as independence is left behind. This feels uncomfortable all round, but can also be a very positive life process – another phase of growing up.

Updating family relationships

So how does this idea of setting suitable boundaries work out in the face of change?

If one or both parents have always been loving and generous, you might find yourself swamped by loss when it's your turn to look after them. Maybe dementia has cost your Dad his clear view of you as a beloved son or daughter, or your Mum is so hard pressed that she can't spare the energy to look after you any more.

Of course you have a lifetime of good memories to sustain you through the harder parts of caring, but it may also be helpful to take some time to think and pray, laying down the 'Mummy/Daddy/little me' aspect of your relationship with them. They have given you so much, but God will always be your Father who looks after you. Here is an opportunity to take another step into maturity.

Sadly, some parents have always been difficult, and now old age and frailty force closer contact with the family again. Maybe your childhood was affected by alcoholism, addiction or mental illness, or your parents were too selfish, rigid or chaotic to look after you properly. Being around very damaged elderly people can be difficult for anybody, and for a wounded son or daughter the very thought of walking back into that situation can be overwhelming indeed.

The carer dealing with an alcoholic, a mentally ill or a deeply unpleasant parent (or two) obviously needs support to keep going. We are not called to lose our emotional healing and slide into old patterns of fear or excessive sub-mission, although some immature parents may expect their offspring to be under their thumb for ever. *They* may or may not choose to change, but *we* can change and grow with God's help, building and maintaining healthy boundaries in the face of unhealthy attitudes.

Sometimes the relationship gets better as the parent ages. A carer and parent get to know each other very well: old bar-riers can be swept aside and mutual respect leads to a truly mature relationship.

Get real

Do you have up-to-date, realistic expectations of your parent? Perhaps they can no longer nurture you as a person, see their own situation clearly, or manage practical matters such as cooking or personal hygiene. There is only frustration ahead if you keep expecting these things from them.

Mhairi remembers:

> When Mum developed dementia and still lived alone, I found
> it very difficult that she was not caring for her appearance and
> would not let anyone help her. She often looked unkempt, and
> this added another emotional hurdle to deal with on each visit. I
> also did not like the idea that others would think that I was letting
> her down by taking her out looking the way she did.
>
> However, my job involved accepting – just as they were –
> people who, for lots of reasons, were 'different', and I realized
> that I had to be like that with Mum.

Likewise, if a parent has unrealistic expectations of you at any point, you can tackle this more calmly once you are aware of the problem. Your parent may wish you to act in a certain way, but your response (like your attitude) is your business, coming from your side of the fence.

Role reversal in practice

Role reversal impacts on every family in the parent-care years, bringing its own burdens and stresses to a parent/carer relationship. It is sad and deeply unsettling to see a previously strong, independent parent reduced to neediness – or to *be* such a parent, for that matter. It needs careful handling to establish who sets the tune day by day in a parent-caring setting, particularly if the parent is living independently. An ageing parent is likely to be less flexible generally, so the onus is on the carer to serve and lead unobtrusively.

From my own experience as an ill person needing support from carers, the best kind of care leaves me feeling empowered, full of possibilities and choices, yet still my own person. Happily, my illness leaves me in sound mind, so it is sensible to allow me to set the agenda. However, there are many levels of choice in daily life: even a mentally frail person can be given the dignity of choice, be it only which TV channel to watch or what goes into their sandwich.

Finding the right path through role reversal is obviously a delicate matter. Families need to renegotiate over time as abilities decline, as Elisabeth describes here:

> I have found the role reversal surprisingly easy, in the sense
> that I know that it is absolutely right to support my parents in
> the last stages of their lives. That isn't to say that it is *all* easy! I
> have worked very hard to enable both parents to retain as much
> independence as possible for as long as possible.
>
> I think both of them struggled in the early stages with the role
> reversal. My dad found the loss of his abilities agonizing over

a long period, because he was very much the caring provider
for my Mum, but he has always been very appreciative of my
support.

My Mum couldn't accept that their living circumstances were
rapidly becoming impossible, but was totally dependent on me
to keep the ball rolling, while at the same time insisting on doing
things her way. Then, during the final months of my father's
life, my Mum realized that she needed my support and has since
become very grateful for it, acknowledging frequently that she
can't manage without me.

Through all these changes and challenges, we rest on the fact
that God is with us, seeing our efforts as we serve.

Back to square one?

Role reversal should work both ways, but sometimes our
parents miss the boat. Is it possible to be a grown-up when
your parents still see you as a child? What happens if you
move back into your childhood home to care for your
parents? You may need to change the script, in the sense
that your parents may not have noticed or accepted that you
grew up a while back.

The close bonds and intimate boundaries between young
children and their parents are meant to change over time.
Teenagers try their wings, leave home and become independent adults. If marriage happens, the new marriage
partner takes first place in the other's affection, and parents
are no longer central. If parents fail to accept this natural
process at any point, it puts unfair pressure on all concerned,
and family closeness may be affected.

When frail parents eventually need support, the process of
change enters a new phase. Some parents may then seek to
draw a caring son or daughter back into outdated patterns.

This pressure must be resisted, however difficult it feels, to allow the carer space to work effectively and happily.

Standing your ground

You could start by actively changing your part in the script, if it's not a good one. Think through and then act out a confident, calm approach which makes it respectfully clear that you are an adult. It can be a pleasant surprise to see how well Dad responds. If he doesn't respond so well, you will know that you are being a mature adult in the situation, and persistence may yet prevail. Some carers choose to call their parents by their first names to mark a fresh start, away from the old child/Mum/Dad pattern of relating.

As for living in the family home, you are up against the power of memories. Time travel is alive and well in your childhood bedroom. How about redecorating, or removing the toy collection on the bookshelf? These things are powerful symbols of childhood that could rewind you forty years every time you go in there.

Another problem with moving back in is the way others may view it. Men are at risk of being seen as a mummy's boy, and either sex can find themselves strangely invisible. People ask the carer how their parent is, but may forget that the carer also has needs and hopes. Time off for a hobby or with friends is not a luxury but a vital necessity for a live-in carer.

Space to breathe

A frail parent may not understand the need for his carer to have a break without him. This is a bit like a toddler who can't see why he has been left behind with Granny, while Mum and Dad have a romantic weekend away. In both cases the person being cared for lacks insight. He will benefit from fresh, cheerful carers, and should not be allowed to veto this necessary respite.

But it's very hard for a carer to push for time off respectfully against the wishes of a parent. Many elderly people dislike changes in routine so, once a regular slot is set up, the grumbles may diminish. Even if they refuse to approve, remember that nobody else works constantly without time off, and rest and space are absolutely necessary for carers to continue in their work. It is not neglectful or unloving to find a suitable care set-up and leave an unwilling parent behind for a short period, since the overall aim is to enable the carer to continue to give care.

Manipulation

'But I promised your mother she'd never go into a home.'

'I don't want strangers in the house.'

'I don't like those frozen meals. I like proper home cooking.'

'But I can't afford a carer.'

'I can always change my will, you know.'

Frail elderly parents can attempt to get their own way by underhand means when they feel under threat by poor health or the prospect of loneliness. They may always have been manipulative, or perhaps now that they are not able to manage their own lives, they are trying to regain a sense of control. The root is fear, frustration and insecurity, but such behaviour is very hard to handle.

Now add in a spouse, other relatives, neighbours and health-care professionals to misinform of the situation, and things can get really lively! Of course accurate information sharing can head off some of this, and good relationships between an old person's carers can offset it.

Making changes to take pressure off a parent, if possible,

may improve manipulative behaviour by reducing the under-lying stress.

Promise me . . .

Making promises under pressure is a recipe for resentment, yet it can be very hard to respond graciously to demands for promises without ending up in a bind. One way round this is to say, 'I respect you too much to lie to you, or to make a promise I may not be able to keep. I will promise always to care for you and do my best to make sure you are all right.' Another approach is to say you will have to think it over and answer later. Very few situations call for an instant answer.

It is worth prayerfully rehearsing a healthy response to a manipulative parent's favourite strategies, as we saw earlier in dealing with parents who still see you as a child. The truth is that you *can* rethink the script, and if you change your lines, the whole scene changes too. This brings together the principles of living within your God-given boundaries and choosing your own attitudes and behaviour. God's principles are very powerful, and the results may truly surprise you.

The bottomless pit

Some parents have such high and inflexible expectations that nothing will ever be enough. They may be selfish, strug-gling with loss of independence, finding any change hard, or perhaps fearful of abandonment, but the result is truly soul-destroying for the carer. If direct negotiation fails, the only alternative is to decide for yourself how much is enough and try to stick to it.

Accusations of neglect can be countered by keeping a diary of contact and gently pointing out that you phoned three days ago, were in this morning, or whatever. Dementia sufferers are naturally prone to feeling neglected if they forget your visit, but a photo taken of them with you at family occasions, with the date added, saves them worrying later about having missed it.

Understanding sour attitudes in old age

Some elderly people are a joy to be around, always outward-looking and positive. Others struggle to be gracious (or even polite) as age-related decline kicks in. 'Why is she so negative these days?' you wonder. 'She never used to be this way.' Here are some factors to consider.

Making allowances all round

Old age doesn't come alone. If only people could simply ease into their final years without pain, acute illness, deafness, dementia or other difficulties. As carers, we are not immune to the effects of such illness, and this can directly affect our relationships with our parents.

For example, dementia or other illnesses affecting the brain can transform a parent's personality and behaviour, which is obviously going to affect the family. It is truly painful and unnerving to see your own mother or father change into someone you don't recognize, or even someone who fails to recognize you. The carer needs time to reflect and grieve over what is lost in order to care effectively for their parent now (more on handling dementia in Chapter 7).

Some disabilities directly affect communication, such as deafness or speech difficulties. It's easy to see why things get tense for Julie and her Mum at times:

> I particularly feel stressed by our communication difficulties, as Mum is increasingly deaf and refuses to get help. I become hoarse trying to communicate. Also her memory loss leads to confusion

and a refusal to accept she has said or done things, leading to anger on her part, and difficulty for me.

It's no wonder that relating to a changing parent can be so exhausting at times. As we make allowances for our ill parents, we need to understand that the effect of their illnesses on us is part of the load we carry.

The impact of major health problems

Maybe your parent is struggling with the limits of poor health on daily life. My biggest health decline some years ago was a huge challenge to face, despite loving care and good support. Here's how it felt for me:

I started to go out only rarely, pushed in a wheelchair instead of walking on my own, which I found embarrassing at first. I still hate crossing the road under someone else's judgment. Frustration became routine as I could no longer buy a last-minute birthday present, nip out for a pint of milk, or reliably cook a meal. I never felt well, pain-free or energetic. My enjoyable work, hobbies and church activities were lost wholesale, so I was bored, yet lacked the energy to do anything.

I felt shy, diminished and substandard. Going to bed at 9pm, plus a compulsory afternoon nap, made me feel like a small child again, and the endless planning to get ordinary things done became tiring and annoying. No cure was available, and the doctors were unhelpful. Pain added a layer of grumpiness, and I found it hard to rise above my low mood as the months turned to years without improvement. Oh yes, and I got fat!

Looking outwards, my social life wilted as many friends fell away, daunted by my obvious suffering and my preoccupation with illness and loss. The friends who understood me best were the ones facing their own health mountains, so contact was limited. Social visits had to be squeezed into my own unpredictable timetable, since I was so easily tired. Spontaneity was no longer possible.

My relationship with God was not immune: I felt angry, resentful and unwanted, like a dog sent to its basket in disgrace.

> *Life with a major illness is a marathon that doesn't seem to have a finishing line*

I was not easy to be around as I grieved my losses, yet I needed the chance to share my burden. I still have my moments. Life with a major illness is a marathon that doesn't seem to have a finishing line.

Could your crabby parent be facing some of these issues? Just because she's old doesn't make it any easier, and in fact I think my youth helped me to be flexible, look forward and get creative over practical limitations. Also, I had a lot of love and sympathy because a younger person in a wheelchair is obviously poorly. An old person may find their new and distressing limitations taken for granted by others.

In time the pain of my situation eased as I recovered from the shock, so that, although I am still limited, I do enjoy life again. I hope this will also happen for you and your parents, but please try to be patient with yourself and them. It does take time to adjust to loss.

Handling privacy
Sharing details about an old person
We owe our parents respect when handling their personal information, yet we are likely to need a safe place to share our own struggles as carers. Family members can let off steam together, or perhaps a discreet friend could be the right person to listen.

If your parents are both alive, one may want to unload on to you specific details of the other's decline, which can be painful or embarrassing to hear. Yet this difficult service of listening offers a vital safe place for your Mum as she struggles with her partner's changing health.

Telling the truth in love

As we liaise with various professionals or other family members, we may find ourselves in muddy waters. We need to tell the truth to get much-needed help, but our parents may wish to disguise or deny their decline. Caring relatives can be under a lot of pressure to collude in denial, but may see clearly that this is getting in the way of important things such as safety, health or hygiene.

One way around this is privately to ring or arrange a visit to discuss the true picture with a parent's doctor, social worker or whoever, and then ask them to maintain your parent's sense of privacy by not letting them know that the information has been shared. This needs some thought: will it lead to more denial and evasion between you and your parent? Would it be better to come clean? Key is the aim of preserving dignity and keeping an attitude of respect, and this will work out differently in each situation. While doctors are not free to disclose patient details, they are usually happy to hear useful information, and to respect your wish for a confidential chat about Mum or Dad.

Your own privacy

It can be hard to know how much to withhold when a parent has little else to think about but your activities and friends. Perhaps you are their only regular contact apart from the TV, and they are understandably hungry for a slice of life. This is a particular problem for parents whose friends or other relatives have died, leaving them isolated and bored.

As your parents have been around since you were born, they feel they know you inside out, even if they don't. This can lead to a lack of respect for you and your privacy. They may feel they have a right to know everything you do, or to take over your time with your friends, particularly if you live with them. The carer can find himself carefully protecting a core of privacy against his parents. It is possible to be too close to a parent, and this is not helpful, loving or healthy.

It can help to save up snippets of local news or current events to discuss, thereby shifting the focus away from you. In this way, you are still meeting the need for fresh topics of conversation.

The substitute spouse

Another issue pops up when a parent dies or becomes ill, and the grieving partner transfers some of the functions of a spouse on to a son or daughter. The carer now becomes a substitute spouse. Obviously sexual approaches are unacceptable, but there are more subtle invasions of emotional privacy that feel wrong to the carer, while the parent is perhaps unaware of any problem.

Examples of this are sharing very personal details or feelings, expecting too much personal information from the carer, or perhaps giving overbearing hugs. In this situation, the carer is not being unloving in marking out healthy boundaries, for example, changing the subject, or moving gently out of an uncomfortable embrace. The alternative is a damaged relationship, which will not help anybody. In fact, allowing this behaviour to continue blocks your parent's normal process of grieving and prevents them from moving on into recovery.

People who lose their spouse may also lose the person who touched them the most. A carer can fill a heartfelt need simply by holding Dad's hand, and also head off less acceptable needy behaviour.

Boundaries that set us free

So how did Jesus find focus and peace in the face of endless, conflicting demands on his time and attention? Mark 1 describes the busy time when Jesus began his preaching and healing ministry and became a local 'celebrity'. The next day his disciples were literally caught napping:

> Very early in the morning, while it was still dark, Jesus got up, left the house and went off to a solitary place, where he prayed. Simon and his companions went to look for him, and when they found him, they exclaimed: 'Everyone is looking for you!' Jesus replied, 'Let us go somewhere else – to the nearby villages – so that I can preach there also. That is why I have come.' So he travelled throughout Galilee, preaching in their synagogues and driving out demons.
> (Mark 1:35–39)

If Jesus had just stayed put and waited for breakfast, his day would have been taken over by the urgent needs of those around him. By putting his Father first, Jesus was reminded that his time was not his own, nor did it belong to whoever shouted the loudest.

Although the disciples wanted Jesus to come back and help the needy crowds waiting anxiously at the door, he felt free to move on to minister elsewhere. He knew who he was and what he was called to do. He was in charge of living out his unique destiny under God's command, and he didn't allow anybody to derail him or manipulate him into turning aside.

His firm grasp of his ordained task gave him confidence to serve, even if others disagreed with his priorities.

Jesus is our model as we try to live healthy, balanced lives through a season of competing needs and strong personalities. Like him, we need to find time for God's overview to keep us on track with a sense of our true calling.

To ponder

1. What factors have set your view of yourself in the past? Do you think you see yourself as God sees you?

2. Do you think your relationship with your parent has been changed by role reversal? By illness? Is it better or worse overall?

3. Is your parent manipulative at times? Does he or she have unrealistic expectations of you? How do you handle these pressures?

'Don't hold your parents up to contempt. After all, you are their son, and it is just possible that you may sometimes take after them.' Evelyn Waugh

'Daughter am I in my mother's house, but mistress in my own.' Rudyard Kipling

Active engagement with life is a key component in successful ageing – final conclusion of medical researchers,

Bowling and Dieppe, after reviewing many research papers on ageing [2]

Lord, make me an instrument of your peace,
Where there is hatred, let me sow love;
where there is injury, pardon;
where there is doubt, faith;
where there is despair, hope;
where there is darkness, light;
where there is sadness, joy;
O Divine Master,
grant that I may not so much seek to be consoled as to console;
to be understood, as to understand;
to be loved, as to love.
For it is in giving that we receive;
it is in pardoning that we are pardoned,
and it is in dying that we are born to eternal life.
St Francis of Assisi

6. Why do I feel this way? Working with difficult emotions

Many parent-carers struggle with difficult emotions, yet feel they should be above such feelings as loving sons and daughters, and as Christians too. Well, welcome to the world of parent-caring. It's a good thing to do, but sometimes it feels bad.

If you skipped to this chapter first, then let's recap . . . We've already established some scriptural principles to help carers with painful emotions. Chapter 2 looked at how to handle the life changes that parent-care brings. Chapter 3 looked at stress and how to vent difficult emotions, and Chapter 5 tackled boundaries and privacy. Then we established principles to help to nurture a healthy emotional life, even when the going gets tough. On that foundation, we'll take a closer look at three major emotional issues for carers: embarrassment, guilt and worry.

Handling embarrassment

Nobody seems to talk about feeling embarrassed as a carer, yet it comes to us all at some point. We may wince as others react unkindly to our unwell parents, or blush at the more personal tasks, like dressing, bathing or toileting. We may feel uncomfortable delving into our parent's finances or knowing the details of their illnesses. Our parents themselves may feel embarrassment over the same issues. All these things will feel worse initially, usually becoming easier with time, but other issues may then arise. Embarrassment can be a significant unseen drain on scarce energy.

Did you ever wonder why doctors and nurses don't get embarrassed? It is not an inborn grace, that's for sure. I confronted major embarrassment at medical school when I realized I was going to have to find a way to put strangers at ease, before asking them a series of extremely personal questions and examining them all over. I was nineteen and a nice Christian girl, and I needed a strategy fast.

As I prayed and puzzled over this, I realized that it was my job to set the tone for my encounters with patients. I went out of my way to act in a friendly, professional and welcoming way, regardless of my feelings, and the patients responded well. As I acted like a professional, my reactions altered to fit my behaviour. My own embarrassment receded promptly, and so did theirs. Looking back, I can see that I redrew my personal boundaries to suit my new work situation and chose to behave as I hoped to feel.

Behind closed doors

Of course it's different if it's your relative, but someone needs to take charge of the atmosphere, and it might as well be you. The poor woman has enough to deal with, having to be taken to the toilet for the first time since she was a toddler.

How would you feel if this was you? What would you hope for in an attendant? Personally, I would like someone who was calm, and not obviously embarrassed. If you feel bad, try acting, as I did on the wards as a teenager. Make *her* the focus, pin on a smile, and pretend you are happy to deal with this new experience. Then at least she is not unsettled by your negative reactions. This will also help you get a grip on your feelings.

This acting strategy also comes in very handy if you feel irritated or stressed by a parent's behaviour, be it slow, repetitive or plain unreasonable. Try pretending you are acting in a soap opera, which is going out live and being watched by millions across the country. Your part is that of a devoted son or daughter, caring for your relative, no matter what they do or say. You don't win any awards for your inner feelings, just your ability to play the part.

Acting the part

I know this idea may sound stupid and trivial, but acting a part really can work. It may even strike you as dishonest at first, but in fact it's the reverse: it is deliberately choosing to be a better person. Remember Colossians 3:12 from Chapter 5? '. . . clothe yourselves with compassion, kindness, humility, gentleness and patience.' We can choose to put on loving, appropriate behaviour, just like choosing to put on a suitable outfit. Once we decide to act out how we want to feel, the feelings start to change.

I used this acting idea to great effect when I had a wailing new baby and a jealous toddler to juggle. Lunchtimes seemed to be daily flashpoints for all three of us. As I acted out the part of a calm, happy soap-opera mum, serving up lunch despite chaos and noise, I felt better, and the children responded well too. Just dropping my tense shoulders, calming my breathing and using a gentle tone of voice made a surprising difference to us all.

I also spent some time thinking about our lunchtime glitch, and decided that filling lunchboxes the night before would get us past the point where I needed about six hands. This simple change worked well, although lunchtimes were still a challenge.

Anybody can address recurring problems by thinking creatively, and perhaps you could try settling a grumpy or embarrassed parent by showing calm behaviour and speech.

Handling guilt

I've never yet met a parent-carer who didn't have feelings of guilt. Whether we live in or out, give care day and night, or visit once a month, we all tend to feel guilty: we're not doing it right, not doing enough, or we're doing it so well that we're neglecting other people.

Why this epidemic of guilt?

- The devil hates those who obey God; this is one of his major attack points.
- Christians in particular may feel they should not ignore or suppress guilt.
- People who take up the challenge of caring for parents tend to be conscientious types.
- Parents decline, despite our best efforts, becoming ever more needy over time.
- Parent-caring lacks clear limits, so we could always be doing that little bit more.
- Exhaustion leaves us in an emotional fog, unable to assess our situation properly.
- Guilt and worry often feed off each other.

Guilt is important because, like all unresolved emotional pressures, it drains the owner day in, day out. We really need to get a grip on this in order to give of our best.

So why do I feel guilty?

The Bible tells us about two very different sources of guilty feelings called conviction and condemnation, and gives clear instructions about handling each.

Conviction is 'meaningful guilt', a blessing from God, specific to one clear issue. It drives us to act and shows us what to do. The feelings of guilt are resolved as soon as the issue is sorted out. Here's an example:

'If you really keep the royal law found in Scripture, "Love your neighbour as yourself," you are doing right. But if you show favouritism, you sin and are convicted by the law as law-breakers' (James 2:8–9).

James is holding the church to account for treating the rich better than the poor. He gives a specific instruction from God's law and shows them how they have fallen short. Their path to recovery is clear, and he has not withdrawn his concern from them, although they are in the wrong. It hurts, but it is also for their good.

Condemnation, 'toxic guilt', is the devil's ploy. It hangs like a dark cloud, leaving a feeling that we are bad and always will be. There is no clear way of escape: trying harder or making changes does not improve matters, and we drag along, feeling awful indefinitely. Nobody was ever harmed by conviction, but condemnation is damaging indeed, and the Bible teaches us to resist it along with other types of satanic attack. Paul spells it out: 'Therefore, there is now no condemnation for those who are in Christ Jesus, because through Christ Jesus the law of the Spirit of life set me free from the law of sin and death' (Romans 8:1–2).

As believers, we have the great privilege and joy of being freed from the burden of our sin through Jesus. What a pity to allow the devil to enslave us again with false feelings of guilt.

As believers, we have the great privilege and joy of being freed from the burden of our sin through Jesus. What a pity to allow the devil to enslave us again with false feelings of guilt

Truth and lies

Here are three common lies that trap us in condemnation, along with their antidotes.

1. I have all these bad thoughts, so I must be bad

The devil may convince us that a bad thought or impulse is our fault, whereas in fact it's temptation, which is his department, not ours. There is no need to feel guilty or to repent over temptation. Just kick the thought out straightaway, and keep kicking if it returns.

2. I am a sinful person and a bad carer

First of all, we're human, so we're all sinful, but your sins are confessed to God and covered by the blood of Jesus, aren't they?

Next, stop and think: would you judge another carer in your shoes as harshly as you're judging yourself? We are commanded to love our neighbour as ourselves, which says to me that God expects us to love, forgive and care for our own selves. Some are so caught up with self-hatred that they reject God's amazing creation and his work – in their own lives. If you find yourself thinking this way a lot, you might be depressed and need medical help.

3. **I should do more to meet my parent's needs**

Try to be objective, even if you are overtired. Actually, if you're overtired, you're probably overworking, not under-performing at all. The key is to find the OFF switch and use it whenever you can, even if it's only for a three-minute break between jobs. The OFF switch is helpfully labelled:

> *I have stopped working*
> *Good for me!*
> *I'm going to relax now*

Also, don't confuse 'Mum needs more help' with '*I* must do more for Mum.' Share the care, please.

Handling worry

It's a pity that worrying is a complete waste of time, because here's me with a natural talent for it. How about you? Some people feel guilty if they *aren't* worrying over their old folks, and indeed there may appear to be plenty to worry about. The problem is that worrying blocks faith, paralyses action and erodes peace and confidence. Worry is not loving or helpful. Concern leading to action is a healthier substitute, with a helping of trust in our God who holds the future. I'm not suggesting that it's easy to stop worrying, but worry is harmful, and it's not inevitable.

Some unfortunate carers develop an illness called 'clinical anxiety', with or without depression. If your anxiety gets out of hand under the heavy stress of caring for parents, please seek professional help before things get any worse. Carers need to keep fit in order to be effective, and there are plenty of good techniques available for anxiety management. Start with an honest chat with your doctor and ask what is on offer. The strategies below will also be useful.

Sinless perfection for beginners

We know that sinless perfection is impossible to attain during this life. This sad fact shouldn't stop us from co-operating with God, trying to live out good behaviour while resisting sinful behaviour. Worry is a good example of an area where many of us have to persist. We can only start from where we are, not from where we'd like to be. From here on, we can learn, practise, try hard and make progress over time. Some, like me, have a natural tendency towards worrying, where others have weaknesses in other areas.

The devil would love it if we all lay around weeping over our failures rather than repenting, getting up and trying again. Perfectionism dressed up as humility says, 'If I can't get it 100% right, there's no point in trying; I'm too sinful to succeed.' We need to be willing to put the past in God's hands every day and press on towards our goal. This approach shows real humility and gets results.

Overcoming worry

Well, how do we begin? Returning to the passage we looked at in Chapter 3, here is some straight talk about worry:

> Do not be anxious about anything, but in everything, by prayer and petition, with thanksgiving, present your requests to God. And the peace of God, which transcends all understanding, will guard your hearts and your minds in Christ Jesus.
> (Philippians 4:6–7)

I love the word 'but'. We are not expected to stop worrying and somehow 'just cope', but instead to *replace* our worry with a trusting relationship with God. This relationship will bring us peace and strength to guard against the temptation to relapse into renewed worry. God's help frees us to choose a better way.

Paul tells us to pray and ask with thanksgiving, which may feel like a chore to start with, but it gives a better perspective. 'Count your blessings' is a good tactic when you're worried, because it keeps you focused on talking to God rather than drifting into rehashing your worries.

If you find this drift from prayer to worry happening a lot, try this. Imagine your worries as one of those annoying flashing adverts that pop up in a box on your computer screen, distracting you from what you're trying to do. Every time you realize you are back to worrying, imagine yourself clicking the worry box closed, so that you can see the prayer screen properly. You may have to keep closing those boxes over and over again, but that's fine. You have no obligation to give them your attention right now. If you don't use computers, imagine choosing to ignore a roadside advertisement to allow you to concentrate on your driving.

Next, in every circumstance we are to present our requests to God. We've already discovered that telling God all our concerns brings release from emotional stress. This process builds a stronger relationship with the Father, and also makes room for his peace to fill us up. In this way we can turn worry to our advantage, because it drives us to prayer.

Some of us have confused worry with love. Your parents don't need, or want, you to worry yourself to death. What they want is to know that you are taking a loving interest. If you phone up feeling frantic, you are unlikely to give them much in the way of support. They need you to be calm and sensible.

Elisabeth admits:

> I do worry. And I'm sorry that I'm so slow to learn that our great
> big God is well able, not only to deal with the whole scheme of
> things, but to give me all the wisdom, patience and strength I
> need.

Kicking the habit

Jesus taught in Matthew 6:25–34 that we don't need to worry
about our material needs because of God's loving provision.
His closing comment gives us a strategy to tackle worries
of all kinds: 'Therefore do not worry about tomorrow, for
tomorrow will worry about itself. Each day has enough
trouble of its own' (Matthew 6:34). Jesus understood the way
worries seep from the issue at hand to blot out the whole
of life. He tells us here to keep to the point in our thoughts,
instead of allowing ourselves to go on a world tour of things
that could go wrong one day.

If constant worry about your parents has become a way of
life, you might need to think about ways to break the habit.
For instance, give yourself a short appointment for worry,
and stick to it. It sounds unlikely, but it really works. Worry
about this issue is only allowed at 9am for fifteen minutes,
or whatever suits your day, but try for a morning slot to
avoid going to bed with it. When you start to worry at other
times, tell yourself firmly, 'It's not the time now. I will worry
about that at 9am.' If you are busy and miss your slot, it has
to wait until tomorrow. During the fifteen minutes, let it rip
in God's presence, and then move on. The worry, amazingly
enough, shrinks to fit, and stops overshadowing the whole
day and half the night. As the habit of worrying is broken,
confidence grows that change is possible. We're now on the
move!

It's too important not to laugh

Coming from another angle, the late Selwyn Hughes, Christian writer and counsellor, devised a delightful two-part cure for worrying. First, consider your situation. Now, if you had the choice, would you rather be in your situation or be eaten by a crocodile? If this fails, it's time for part two. Would you rather be in your situation or be *half* eaten by a crocodile?

Hmm, I thought so.

It's worth seeking out books, people, cartoons or films that make you laugh. Look for moments of humour in your day, however black, and save them up to tell others or remember later. Laughter is a powerful weapon against worry, self-pity, resentment and depression too.

Unmasking the lies

The devil plots to bind us up in worries and fears, but there is hope. Psalm 124 tells the story of a great victory won over well-armed enemies and crippling fears:

If the LORD had not been on our side –
  let Israel say –
if the LORD had not been on our side
  when men attacked us,
when their anger flared against us,
  they would have swallowed us alive;
the flood would have engulfed us,
  the torrent would have swept over us,
the raging waters
  would have swept us away.
Praise be to the LORD,
  who has not let us be torn by their teeth.
We have escaped like a bird
  out of the fowler's snare;

the snare has been broken,
    and we have escaped.
Our help is in the name of the LORD,
    the Maker of heaven and earth.

Worry can make us lose all sense of perspective, as King David describes so vividly in verses 1–5. Worry about a specific problem turns into a feeling that we will literally be swept away and never seen again. We can almost feel the water closing in overhead. Worry has turned to fear, and fear to panic.

David goes on to explain that, without God's help, they would all have met a violent death. God saved them from a situation that David compares to a great flood, wild animals with sharp teeth and finally a fowler (a bird catcher) equipped with a deadly snare to catch and kill his victims. This is horror-movie stuff. David obviously had a vivid imagination.

God did more for Israel that day than snatch them from the jaws of death. He also broke the fowler's snare so that it could never be used to trap or hurt them again. This was a long-term victory for the people of God that teaches us powerful principles to use against fears and worries today.

For example, a caring daughter may fear the death of a parent. Hours are spent (wasted) in trying to foresee every need or crisis ahead of time, yet somehow the subject just grows and takes root in her mind. She feels that, if her fear comes true, she will go under, and she knows that death will happen some day. She is paralysed and dragged down by fear, and so is missing her opportunities to serve and enjoy her parents now, never mind ruining other aspects of her life. Her parents are not immortal; they are old and frail. Isn't it true to say that what she fears will happen?

Truth
+ lie
_____
= problem

Her perspective is true in part, but it also contains a fatal flaw. Yes, it's true that her parents will eventually die, but she doesn't need to be swept away by it. The devil's lie is that such a circumstance will be the end of her, and she will surely be overwhelmed. Millions of people all over the world are held captive by this same fear, that some circumstance will sweep them away and destroy them. The circumstance changes, but the underlying problem is the fear of being totally destroyed by adversity.

Truth
− lie
_____
= solution

Fear of destruction can be broken by using two keys to lasting freedom, found in verse 7:

'We have escaped like a bird out of the fowler's snare; the snare has been broken, and we have escaped.'

Here are the key truths:

1. God is on our side to help us escape when we cry to him in trouble.
2. God has broken the snare, and so has permanently destroyed the devil's weapon against us.

How do we find lasting freedom from fear, in the face of life's troubles and the devil's subtle attacks? It looks far less scary when it's broken down into chunks. First, there's the actual thing we fear, such as losing a parent. This will be hard to face, but most people do face it, survive it and grow stronger. Then there's the underlying fear that we will be swept away. This one is a whopper from the devil, the father of lies. God's grace is always available to us and far bigger than any trauma we may live through. God will never leave us nor forsake us. He has placed our feet upon a rock. As we declare and give thanks for this truth, the fowler's snare is broken in our lives.

Truth
– 2 × lie
_____

= final solution

Next, we need to choose to walk in freedom, even when the devil regroups and tries another tack. This fresh lie is that we are still bound by fear and are forced to react as we did before. The truth is that we are now free. Those all-too-familiar feelings of fear are nothing but temptation, which can be resisted with the help of God's Word. Remember, because the snare is broken, it has no further power, unless we permit it.

The best response is to use verse 7 to declare the truth. Bring it to mind, or try saying it aloud, if privacy allows: 'The snare is broken and I am free!' Jesus himself spoke Scripture aloud to defeat the devil's temptations (Matthew 4:1–11), so it's a good strategy to follow.

This is hard work, like breaking a bad habit, but the benefit is obvious: freedom from unmanageable fear. The specific thing we fear is not the issue, but the underlying process of fearfulness, so it's worth sorting it out now to avoid dealing with it again and again over different concerns.

This process may play out over a period of time, with skilled support, counselling and prayer, or it may happen in a single moment of truth. Either way, the result is well worth the effort.

For King David, as for us, this particular victory did not end all enemy attacks. Hard times will surely come, and the devil will try his luck in every season of life. However, God is committed to us and to our freedom. He will not allow us to be held by fears, unless we give in to temptation and let those fears take root. Even if we fall back, he will forgive us and help us to break free again.

God with us

As we wrestle with our emotions, it helps to know that God doesn't expect us to go through life with a noble smile, come what may. King David was a man after God's own heart. In Psalm 56 he pours forth his outrage, anger, fear, hatred, worry, complaints and tears before God, without any fear of disapproval. In fact he looks to his loving Father to receive and respect his feelings: 'Record my lament; list my tears on your scroll – are they not in your record?' (Psalm 56:8).

David knew that God's presence was the safest place in which to lay down the burden of difficult feelings, and that the God who made us is not surprised by human reactions. This understanding helped David to run towards a finishing line of thanksgiving, despite his suffering and his own imperfections: 'I am under vows to you, O God; I will present my thank-offerings to you. For you have delivered me from death and my feet from stumbling, that I may walk before God in the light of life' (Psalm 56:12–13).

To ponder

1. Do you sometimes find yourself embarrassed, cross or flustered while dealing with your parent? Try one day of acting out how you would like to feel and behave, and see how it goes.

2. Do you feel guilty today? Think it over. Is it toxic guilt, or meaningful guilt? What reaction is needed from you?

3. Do you find that worries can get out of proportion at times? What do you think about the strategies in this chapter?

'I have been through some terrible things in my life, some of which actually happened.' Mark Twain

'I have chosen you and have not rejected you. So do not fear, for I am with you; do not be dismayed, for I am your God. I will strengthen you and help you; I will uphold you with my righteous right hand.' Isaiah 41:9–10

'God grant me the serenity to accept the people I cannot change, the courage to change the one I can, and the wisdom to know it's me.' Anon

7. Hi Mum, it's your daughter: Coping with memory loss

Many elderly people are affected by memory loss and, as people now tend to live longer, this problem is sadly growing. Memory problems bring wide-ranging losses to those affected: they trigger unwelcome changes in all directions, and pose huge challenges to parent and carer alike, throwing up deep and painful problems to do with personal worth, safety, relationships, and planning for the future.

Caring for a parent with dementia is a very hard job to do well. Along with the difficulties and frustrations of the day-to-day work, there is the added burden of overseeing the decline while remembering how things used to be. Broken nights are often a feature, and days off may be rare, so exhaustion is a constant threat. Affected families are in daily need of God's grace and strength to see them through this long-term crisis.

It always helps to have vision for the task ahead, so that's our starting point. What is God's perspective on dementia, and how does he want us to handle the person with this devastating illness?

Where have they gone?

Dementia and other major brain malfunctions raise deep issues about the nature of self. What or who makes a person human? If memory, speech and other basic abilities are gone, is the person still a person? Where have they gone while their body lives on?

It helps to consider how we got to this point. Genesis 1 teaches us that humans were made carefully in the image of God and also blessed by him. God knows and cares for each person, although the fall of Adam in Genesis 3 has brought sin, sickness and sorrow into every human life.

Although our frail bodies have a sell-by date, there is spiritual potential built into each person that can blossom into eternal life. Here is Paul, teaching the Corinthian church: 'Now we know that if the earthly tent we live in is destroyed, we have a building from God, an eternal house in heaven, not built by human hands' (2 Corinthians 5:1). Paul compares human bodies to tents: temporary homes for their spirits during their earthly lives. Camping has its limitations, compared to living in a proper house. Likewise, our earthly bodies are prone to weakness and will eventually decline and die, releasing the redeemed spirit to rise to Heaven.

Hidden treasure

These two principles, that God created and cares for each person, and that people have a visible body and a hidden spirit, help us to respect a person with dementia. With this illness, the mind fails first, the body too is affected, and finally the person dies. However, the spirit is not necessarily affected by problems of the body and mind: 'Therefore we do not lose heart. Though outwardly we are wasting away, yet inwardly we are being renewed day by day' (2 Corinthians 4:16).

Dementia damages a person's appearance and abilities, but the inner self remains unchanged and is intimately known to God: 'The LORD does not look at the things man looks at. Man looks at the outward appearance, but the LORD looks at the heart' (1 Samuel 16:7b).

Speech and ability are not necessary for love, joy and satisfaction, as any baby will teach you. A newborn's pure gaze speaks powerfully of the presence of God, uncomplicated by human understanding. Similarly, an outwardly unresponsive, severely disabled person's spirit may be burning brightly. I'm not trying to deny the great loss and suffering caused by dementia, but pointing out that some parts remain unseen and undamaged. A person with advanced dementia is wounded but is still fully human.

Identity crisis

When my son was one day old, he ate a lot, waved his fists and screamed for attention. He had a cross, red face, no manners, little hair and lacked toilet training. He was an unproductive and demanding little scrap, not to mention the trouble we had in persuading him to come out in the first place. Or, to look at it as we did, he was a precious and important Ackerman family member who was wanted, accepted, loved and welcomed by all, just as he was. Although he was so helpless and vulnerable, he deserved and received respect as a fully human person who is a permanent part of our particular family.

At the other end of life, dementia erodes ability, and with it, previously held jobs or roles. The person's identity comes to lie once again in the hands of those around her, be they family or staff. Will they see her as a patient, a burden and a nonentity, or will she remain a beloved wife, a mother and a cherished individual? It's easy to see how this attitude will spill over into if she feels safe, contented and valued day by day, whether living at home or in a residential care facility. This is one of the many reasons why people in care homes still need their relatives to visit them.

As cognitive abilities (thinking, understanding and remembering) decline, the person's relationships must change in order to survive. Intuitive and emotional abilities persist for much longer, and can provide precious moments of mutual tenderness and satisfaction.

Whatever comes, God remains as the eternal, loving Father of the whole human family. Individuals may not remember him, but he will remember, love and hold each one in his heart for ever. A frail old lady with advanced dementia is a person made in the image of God: this alone defines her as a person worthy of respect and attention. This respect underpins and validates all our efforts to do right by those with dementia.

But is it dementia?

The medical side of dementia is too big to cover here, but it's useful to understand the basics. Memory problems in old age are not always due to dementia. Gradual, progressive memory malfunction (confusion) is a symptom that can be caused by dementia or age-related memory loss (ARML), with rarer causes a long way behind. We'll come back to sudden memory loss in a moment.

ARML is a natural consequence of an ageing, less flexible brain, and leads to intermittent memory lapse. It will very slowly progress over decades, leaving the personality intact, and it is not usually a particular problem. Dementia is a serious illness which can strike earlier in adulthood, or more commonly in old age. It has a faster downhill course and wide-ranging effects, including serious, progressive memory loss. Alzheimer's disease is a well-known, common type of dementia.

Sudden confusion in old age, or confusion that suddenly gets worse, is a different issue altogether. It shows there's an acute underlying illness which needs prompt medical attention. It can be a symptom of a physical problem, such as an infection or a drug reaction and, when the problem is treated, the confusion goes back to its previous levels. Another common cause of confusion in the elderly is depression, which may be harder to spot in this age group. Antidepressants can resolve confusion in a depressed older person in just a few weeks. So it's worth having a good look at someone with sudden confusion before assuming that nothing can be done.

Although there is still no cure for dementia, there are drugs available which can now slow down the process of the illness, to enable a higher level of ability than would otherwise be possible for some years to come. Other drug treatments and practical approaches can help to calm an anxious sufferer, and block or damp down hallucinations and other disturbing symptoms. This is one reason why an early diagnosis is worthwhile, even if the prospect of knowing the truth may seem daunting.

Many older people and their families are dogged by fear of dementia, as Jan describes here:

> Mum's memory has deteriorated a little, and she is scared to death of it, and can become quite aggressive when gently told that we have already had that conversation.

If you have a parent with dementia, the commonest types of the illness do not run in the family line, making your own risk of developing dementia no higher than normal. Your doctor can advise about this, but don't let fear overshadow your future for lack of information.

How does dementia start?

Mhairi's Mum developed Alzheimer's disease, a common type of dementia:

> Up to around the age of eighty her memory loss was not very noticeable. But there were little signs like telling me something every time I saw her as though it was news.
>
> On more than one occasion when out shopping she thought the car had broken down and called out her gem of a garage man. He quietly revealed to us that she was just forgetting that the car had a steering lock! However, there was close adherence to familiar routines and she appeared to be coping.
>
> She had always been someone who depended on notes to herself, but very gradually it became clear that the notes were not always acting as a prompt. She would put the 'meal on wheels' in the oven and then forget to eat it.
>
> She must have been aware herself that there was slippage, and she was very good at putting helpful strategies in place. She always carried an envelope in her pocket with her address on it, for example.

Perhaps Mhairi's Mum had ARML in the years before the Alzheimer's kicked in. She obviously had insight into her memory loss at this early stage, and lots of good ideas about managing her difficulties.

Someone whose memory declines more rapidly may have a nervous breakdown due to the burden of 'holding it all together' without insight into what's going wrong. It is worth looking into the causes of an unexpected bout of depression or anxiety in old age, so that any underlying illness can be spotted and help given.

Facing facts

A diagnosis of dementia may come as a surprise, or be a confirmation of what has been seen and feared already for months. Either way, it's a hard knock. But finding out what to expect can help the whole family face up to what lies ahead, though it might be easier to look at the immediate issues and not dwell on the later stages at first. The local community psychiatric nurse can be a great asset here, and a referral can be made by the geriatrician, psychiatrist or family doctor.

Mhairi found the run-up to diagnosis very challenging, a common pattern for families affected by dementia:

> There was a time when no-one really knew exactly what was happening. It was very hard when my mother reacted aggressively. Suddenly she would turn on me and be really unpleasant for no apparent reason. I was so taken aback that sometimes I did not handle it well. I ended up shouting at her once (which I do regret now). It comes out of the severe strain that builds up when you don't understand what you are dealing with. Once I knew it was dementia, and accepted that it was really happening (another difficult transition), I learned to handle it differently.

Mhairi had no professional help or advice in the early stages, perhaps because she was not living in the same area as her Mum. New issues emerged after the diagnosis was confirmed:

We had to face the diagnosis of Alzheimer's and all that this was going to mean, without really having help to know where in the recognized 'stages' she was. No help was given really. All information was gleaned from the Internet.

I was also having to deal with my guilt that I could not be there full-time. We were living 180 miles away, my husband and I working full time, with family still needing our financial support. I know she might have been able to remain at home for longer if I had been close by. Worst of all has been the steady loss of her as she was – the 'long goodbye'.

Comfort in the storm

Caring for a person diagnosed with dementia immediately involves the stress of dealing with their (and your) natural pain and upset over having the illness. It feels like grieving for two people, yourself and your parent. There is likely to be a period of intense grieving all round after the diagnosis, with some recovery over the months as the family settles into the job in hand. However, grieving can be triggered over and over again as the illness progresses.

This New Testament passage highlights the idea of comfort flowing from one to another in the midst of suffering:

> Praise be to the God and Father of our Lord Jesus Christ, the Father of compassion and the God of all comfort, who comforts us in all our troubles, so that we can comfort those in any trouble with the comfort we ourselves have received from God. For just as the sufferings of Christ flow over into our lives, so also through Christ our comfort overflows.
> (2 Corinthians 1:3–5)

Paul shows us the way: when we suffer, it is our privilege to run to our Father for comfort. Once we are filled and nourished by this comfort, we can in turn give comfort to others in trouble. We receive freely and in turn have plenty to give. Trouble comes when we try to be the source of comfort that we ourselves do not possess. This promptly drains us dry and may also fail to meet the need. We can truly minister God's comfort only when our own needs are met by him.

The challenge of dementia care

Caring for a parent with dementia involves daily grieving, as more and more of the person's memories, capabilities and sense of self slip away. It's like standing on the dockside, watching your friend on the deck of a departing ferry boat. You can still see each other, but you are getting further and further apart. His face starts to blur, but you can still see him waving, and then all you can see is the ship moving away.

Dealing with memory loss as a carer means bravely fighting a losing battle, trying to anchor the person in the present while being realistic about the slow loss of self. The actual mechanics of keeping a confused person safe and settled are demanding and frustrating too. It's no wonder that this type of caring is so deeply stressful. It may be easier at times for a son- or daughter-in-law or an unrelated carer to cope with these changes.

A confused person is unlikely to be able to care for those around her. Her focus is increasingly restricted to her own bewildering world. If she happens to be your Mum, this may mean the gradual loss of whatever love and support she has given you in the past, or perhaps occasional flashes of concern along the way. Sadly, in the end, she is unlikely to know who you are, unless another illness ends her life first. Meanwhile, as roles reverse, the carer may feel increasingly protective.

Healthy caring

The job is hard then, but not hopeless: there are plenty of ways for a carer to make a big difference to Mum's quality of life. As we have seen, working yourself into a breakdown is no benefit for anybody, but giving good care can be satisfying. Here are six tried-and-trusted approaches to improving care, that also help to lift some of the emotional burden from the dementia carer.

- Become a high-class carer. There is good information available about your parent's illness and how to handle it, and if you know your stuff, this gives you self-respect and confidence. Some regions have specialized carer courses for dementia, and even supply sitters for the parent left at home.
- Make the most of what's on offer: your parent's health and abilities are likely to be better today than they will be tomorrow, so today's opportunities may not come again. This attitude turns us away from grieving, and moves on to seizing the day, however imperfect.
- Shift your expectation from ability (or its loss) to quality of life day by day. It's very sad to watch someone deteriorate, but it's satisfying to look back on a day or an hour when Mum has been settled, interested, amused or content. Dementia cannot be cured, but it can be well managed, as Mhairi has grasped:

The best bits about caring for Mum are: appreciating things together, like having afternoon tea, a walk in the sunshine, all the beauty around, a flash of memory, the still-present spark of humour, and just being together. I hope that what little I can do is contributing to her quality of life in the circumstances.

- Share the care now; don't wait until you're ill. It is
  not usually possible to 'do it all' as dementia runs
  its downward course, and it is not helpful to limit a
  confused parent's horizons to what one person can
  provide. It is often easier to introduce new people or
  places into Dad's life earlier, while he retains more
  mental flexibility. If an 'indispensable' carer becomes
  ill through lack of time to rest and relax, then major
  upheaval for Dad is inevitable. This is much more
  traumatic than easing him into new routines with
  no rush.
- Celebrate the memories that remain by making a
  memory box, photo album or life-story scrapbook. This
  is useful at home or in a care home, giving Dad a link
  with his previous life events, and an enjoyable topic
  of conversation. Perhaps another helper could record
  Dad's memories and compile the album.[1]
- Respect your parent, while being realistic about his or
  her limits, to help you both feel good.

Respecting a confused parent

It can be hard to preserve daily respect for a confused person
who is losing things like modesty, manners and continence.
It may help privately to give the illness a name of its own.
For example, if you call the dementia Norman, then when
your Dad, Bill, is behaving annoyingly, you can think, 'Oh,
yes, that's Norman again.' It's a true perspective, as Bill
would never behave like this if he were well. This allows you
to separate the person from the illness in your mind, and so
to respect the person and feel what you like about the illness.
As time goes on, there will be more of Norman and less of
Bill, but a surprise appearance can still be savoured.

Another approach is to remember the person as he was in

the past, while caring for him as he is today. At the end of a long life there are many aspects to a person, not all of which are obvious now, but all of which make up the person we see today.

A verse from Proverbs gives us another source of strength: 'A wise son brings joy to his father, but a foolish man despises his mother' (Proverbs 15:20). This verse reminds us that respecting a parent is God's command, and God's commands bring life. Giving this respect to a confused parent helps us to feel that our work is worthwhile, and that we are growing in wisdom. Preserving a parent's dignity, creating a safe, pleasant environment and making the best of what remains intact is a loving, useful task. We can give a sick, vulnerable person a good quality of life within their current limits.

It's a pity that our society gives this caring task and those with dementia such a low priority and so little respect, as Shenaz relates. She makes light of the following episode, but this 'professional' in charge of a care facility is not only clueless about old people, but deeply disrespectful too.

> My Mum was in a residential home for respite care, and the lady in charge wasn't happy with her habits (falling asleep in the afternoon and putting the lumpy food she didn't like on the floor), so the lady gave me a dressing down when I collected my Mum.

Seasons of change
Alongside all the loss, as dementia progresses there is also the odd benefit. People with early dementia tend to become very anxious as they try to hang on to their routines. But as time goes on, they often reach the stage of 'letting go', becoming calmer and allowing others to look after them more easily.

Sadly, this is not true for everyone, but it's worth remembering that dementia is not fixed, with some issues getting easier, even as others bring more trouble. Obsessive behaviour in particular often shifts focus from one topic to another over time.

A person with dementia can also suffer from minor ailments, boredom, over-stimulation, exhaustion or depression, so it helps to attend to these things before blaming every difficulty or mood on dementia. Physical aggression is not a normal, routine part of dementia: common trigger points include the presence of a particular person, and the sheer frustration of not being able to explain what is wrong. The carer turns detective, like a parent handling a pre-verbal toddler's tantrum, trying patiently to identify recurring patterns, and then taking steps to avoid further trouble. A close relationship is obviously a great help here, and the community psychiatric team can also add their expert viewpoint.

Forgetting to take medication or use safety equipment can make other frailties worse so, as confusion deepens, it's important to think about ways to avoid muddles with pills, which can rebound into worsened confusion or serious illness.

Dementia progressively affects clear communication, but a carer can help by speaking clearly and simply. Offer simple ideas and choices to make the most of Dad's abilities. Allow plenty of time for him to notice you're speaking, grasp your meaning and then to respond to you. Try to cut out distractions like the TV playing or someone walking behind you as you speak, because a damaged brain cannot screen out what is not important. Close attention and long familiarity help the carer to grasp the meaning of a word or phrase that may seem irrelevant to a stranger.

Showing love by providing varied smells, tastes, music

and textures engages the senses, sparks memories and brightens up the whole day.

It's helpful to understand the way the illness progresses, so that new features don't take you by surprise. Since there are helplines and courses, fact sheets and books available, why reinvent the wheel? If you are scared of contemplating the later stages of the illness, leave that information out until you need it.

A different kind of memory

Here's a really useful discovery about mental impairment. Research on the damaged brain has shown that, even when the conscious mind cannot remember an event, the emotions do. This is called emotional memory.[2] It's worth making a pleasant experience for someone who cannot remember it later, since they will benefit from the happy or calm feelings as if they had remembered it.

As people with dementia lose intellectual ability, their emotional abilities are often strengthened. This means that Dad will be quick to pick up on body language, expression or tone of voice in those around him, so a calm environment makes a real difference.

Emotions can be strong and upsetting for someone with dementia who can no longer balance feelings with rational thought. A carer can help by expressing what she sees: 'Dad, you look a bit angry. Are you upset because you bumped your head?' This helps the confused person to connect to why he feels a certain way.

Emotional memory and emotional ability can be applied to the faith aspect of care, too. Research has shown that ritual, such as familiar music or prayers, can unlock buried memories and trigger good feelings in dementia sufferers with a personal faith.[3] So it's still worthwhile to take a confused person to church, if possible, even if they can't follow the sermon and promptly forget that they've been there. If they are too ill to go, playing hymns or other familiar music or liturgy, reading Scripture aloud, or simply saying grace may have a calming and faith-building effect. Well-known patterns of belief can reach a confused believer and leave a lingering peace.

As a young doctor, I watched amazed as an apparently comatose, speechless, elderly hospital patient suddenly 'woke up' and sang along – word perfect – to hymns sung by a visiting church team. She even raised her arm and conducted the singing. This was a moving demonstration of emotional memory tapping into long-held patterns of faith.

Give me strength!

As we work hard to care for the confused, we can be confident that God is with us as we serve. Our work has value and purpose to him and to our loved ones. We may be hard pressed and overlooked by the world outside, but God's endless resources are available to us as we care day by day.

> Your love, oh LORD, reaches to the heavens,
>   your faithfulness to the skies.
> Your righteousness is like the mighty mountains,
>   your justice like the great deep.
> Oh, LORD, you preserve both man and beast.
>   How priceless is your unfailing love!
> Both high and low among men
>   find refuge in the shadow of your wings.
>   (Psalm 36:5–7)

To ponder

1. Are you caring for someone with memory problems? If so, what are the most difficult aspects?

2. Do you think that providing a good quality of life for a person with progressive dementia is possible? How do you tackle this in your own situation?

3. Do you have enough support and assistance with your caring work? Do you have anyone to talk to about it?

4. How could the concept of emotional memory change your own caring routines? Write down a few ideas to try out.

5. In your opinion, how does God view a person with advanced dementia? How does he view the act of looking after such a person?

'I've learned that people will forget what you said, people will forget what you did, but people will never forget how you made them feel.' Maya Angelou

'Life is the art of the possible.' Katharine Whitehorn

'Can a mother forget the baby at her breast and have no compassion on the child she has borne? Though she may forget, I will not forget you! See, I have engraved you on the palms of my hands.' Isaiah 49:15–16a

'Every day is an adventure when you have short-term memory loss.' Katrina, eighty-two

'Whatever you are, be a good one.' Abraham Lincoln

8. More needs, changing needs: Finding new ways to care

Transitions and moves in old age are often stressful, perhaps triggered by a crisis of some kind. Panic can set in and guilt can loom large. Since we can't see into the future, it's hard to feel confident when planning ahead.

In fact, setting up more care or moving a parent does not imply failure on anybody's part. It's about being realistic and lovingly responsive to changing circumstances, like good childrearing which makes space for the child to change as he grows up. Finding the best possible solution for a needy old person requires a clear grasp of their current strengths and weaknesses.

The process of moving and resettling can be busy, emotional and draining for all concerned, given the range of points of view in any family, and all the memories tied up in a long-held home.

Many Christians struggle in particular with the idea of their parents going into a care or nursing home, feeling that

such a thing is unscriptural. We'll start by looking at our
position as believing offspring of elderly parents in the light
of God's Word.

God's perspective

So what is our responsibility before God when our parents
become old and frail? Let's have a look at a key passage in
1 Timothy 5, which starts with the radical thought that the
church should take care of needy widows who are without
family support:

> Give proper recognition to those widows who are really in need.
> But if a widow has children or grandchildren, these should learn
> first of all to put their religion into practice by caring for their
> own family and so repaying their parents and grandparents, for
> this is pleasing to God . . .
>
> If anyone does not provide for his relatives, and especially for
> his immediate family, he has denied the faith and is worse than an
> unbeliever.
>
> (1 Timothy 5:3–4, 8)

It is clear that we have a responsibility to make provision,
and to care, for our own elderly relatives. It seems from
the passage that some of these new believers had spotted
a loophole, and had decided to leave the cost and trouble
of providing for their parents and grandparents to their
church. Paul tells them firmly to sort out their bad attitude to their God-given responsibilities and get on with
the job. Caring for family is bound up in the expression
of Christian faith, and cannot be viewed as an optional
extra.

Understanding the context

So what is God saying to us now through this passage? Let's have a look first at the situation at the time. When Paul sat down to write to Timothy, life was very different. With no modern family planning or fast, easy transport, there were larger families who usually lived close to one another, in the area where they had been born. So there would probably have been an extended family conference about Mum when the need arose, and some kind of job-sharing going on, not one person or one small family trying to do it all, alone and unsupported. This cultural pattern saw the needs of the extended family as paramount over the wishes of the individual.

On top of this, there were no state-funded pensions, nor was there free health care. There was no status for lone women, and there were no elder-care facilities of any kind. So it was a straight choice between taking Mum into the family home or seeing her destitute, homeless and begging in the street. I think most of us would know where we stood on that one!

Twenty-first century caring

Our culture has other strengths and weaknesses. We have basic financial provision for the old, and a range of elder-care and health-care facilities. On the other hand, our families tend to be isolated by living far apart, they are smaller, and divorce weakens the ties. These days, more men are in the workplace rather than on the family homestead, and commonly moving across the country to take a new job, and more and more women are out at work. Meanwhile, the achievement culture sends out powerful messages against stopping work for any family reason, leading to poor provision for workers who need flexibility to care for parents. It seems that our brave new world of personal freedom and

It seems that our brave new world of personal freedom and higher living standards has left little room for caring for the weak

higher living standards has left little room for caring for the weak.

As we saw in an earlier chapter, it's hard to pick our path. It feels as if our lives are filled with important and useful things already, without this new task, so where exactly do we go from here?

For the believer, the process of making life choices is informed by an obedient relationship with a loving God, a God who speaks today. As always, God is interested primarily in our heart attitude, and our choices flow on from there. As we assess the past and accept overall responsibility for our elderly parents' well-being, we are released to look at the options available with a healthy and guilt-free perspective.

Handling money

In the context of the challenge of increasing care needs, here are some issues to consider in the area of money:

- Does your parent currently need support in handling finances?
- How will you manage financially if you need to leave, change or cut back on your paid work to take time out to care?
- Can the family afford a decent nursing home or in-house care for as long as it's needed, and is there any state help available? What if the other parent then needs residential care?
- Is it time to sell the unsuitable family home and move your parents to somewhere more manageable?

All this is tricky ground, and careful research and planning are vital to keep family finances within the law and out of the red. Beware of selling a parent's home to a relative, or offering it to them as a gift, as this may lead to legal or tax problems, regardless of motives. For example, your local council will take a very dim view of a parent who tries (or appears to be trying) to avoid care-home fees by hiding or dispersing personal assets. Rules differ according to where you live, but ignorance is no defence, so do please *ask first*.

It's very useful for older couples to have at least some money in a joint account, so that when one of them dies, the survivor has access to the funds to keep them going until the will is settled. Holding assets jointly may also protect against all savings going to pay for one partner's care-home fees, leaving the other partner without resources.

If you're planning to move Mum in with you, the wider family may need to know what's happening about money matters, in order to avoid conflict now or later on. Please don't assume that your brothers and sisters will be happy with whatever arrangement is being made for funding their parents' care and living accommodation. It may affect their own inheritance, for one thing, and they may be feeling left out of the whole process for another. Explaining the options to all concerned at the time can avoid a serious split over money and assets. Perhaps your parents might consider adjusting their wills to reflect the way the money is now moving between them and live-in carers.

Dealing with wills

It can be hard to talk about whether your parent has made a will, can't it? You don't want to appear money-grabbing or nosey, and Mum may not wish to confront the realities of death or discuss her private business. Still, the alternative is

grim. Dying without making a will can leave horrible problems for the next generation, such as long delays in sorting
out the estate, unnecessary tax bills and painful family
disputes.

Some people break the ice by making their own will and
telling their parent about it. Seeing something about wills in
a TV programme or magazine may be another easy opening
for a chat. You can reassure Mum that you don't need to
know what's in her will, but you just want to know that it's
been made, and where to find it when it's needed.

Power of attorney

Power of attorney is a formal agreement for a named person
to handle someone else's affairs, such as signing cheques,
managing bank statements, buying or selling a property,
and so on. It's very useful for those whose parents are
too ill or perhaps too mentally infirm to handle their own
money.

Regulations differ according to where you live, but usually
a suitable form of power of attorney can be mutually agreed
upon and set up with a lawyer at any time, then left on one
side and registered (activated) later on when it's needed. A
cheaper option is to do it yourself, putting together all the
paperwork and registering it by post. Make sure you've got
the right forms for your region and that you've fully understood what's required, as it could be declared void later on if
any aspect is incomplete.[1]

If dementia is diagnosed, this is an obvious time to set up
power of attorney. However, your currently well parent
could be left incapable following a stroke, say, out of the
blue. Power of attorney can be suggested as a useful plan B,
to be set up and then used only as needed.

Both wills and power of attorney are fertile ground for

family quarrels, so consulting all parties is a good way to head this off, if possible.[2]

Living at home

Many people cope well in their own homes as they age, propped up by various services and a relative or neighbour who pops in at intervals. The 'popper-in' has some specific issues to overcome, as well as the usual time-management and role reversal stuff.

What really matters?

Just because your parent needs you to help them deal with a problem doesn't mean that your approach will be the same as theirs. A carer supporting both parents living independently is particularly in need of tact, in addition to a servant-heart attitude. If Mum is propping up Dad and doing the daily stuff, her way of dealing with things needs to take first place wherever possible, even if it means dropping your own standards. For example, keeping the kitchen floor clean is not as important as keeping the couple together at home. If she starts leaving the gas oven on and unlit, or forgetting to eat, then that's a different matter.

The aim is to preserve and respect their way of life and their priorities day to day, while keeping an eye on safety and well-being. This balance requires high-level negotiating skills, and you may not get any thanks for it. She is also a stressed carer, after all, running fast to stand still, worried sick about her husband, and she's eighty-nine to boot.

I stand in awe of tenacious, frail, elderly couples, bravely working, learning and adapting, for love of each other. Sometimes they seem to be propping each other up at a dangerous angle, but somehow they manage to keep going. They are truly worthy of respect and help.

I'm fine, dear

Some old people lack insight about, or deny, how far down-hill things have gone, and therefore see no need for change, however dire things are becoming. The timing of a move is sometimes driven by the exhaustion of caring relatives, even against the wishes of the parent. This can leave the carer cast as the villain. Many a daughter struggles on because she can't face this clash of wills, or because she is trying to honour her parents' unrealistic wishes.

Here is Elisabeth's experience of helping her frail parents to stay on in their own home:

> Mum and Dad's needs gradually increased with age and infirmity, so my input gradually increased, especially after my only sister died three years ago. In the end I had a nervous breakdown. Despite my husband immediately increasing his support for my parents, my illness and hospitalization precipitated a collapse by my Mum. This instantly shot us into the need to find extra care for Mum and Dad, and two months later they moved into a sheltered flat.

It can be hard for a carer to see the situation clearly when she is becoming ever more overworked and exhausted. With hindsight, Elisabeth's parents were only hanging on at home because Elisabeth was working herself into the ground. Her mother, who had early dementia and hence lacked insight, thought they were managing well under their own steam, and so refused to contemplate any change. When Elisabeth's energy was withdrawn, the whole structure fell apart within weeks. Then the move had to be managed at once, while Elisabeth and both parents were acutely ill.

I'm not moving!

For many an old person, their home is their fortress and their comfort blanket. They will naturally fight to keep their way of life. The crunch comes when it is clear that the effort of struggling on at home is too much for them and their support team. It may take time and tact to explore suitable options with them. The sheer effort of going through a lifetime's worth of possessions may be what is holding them back, or perhaps it's fear of the unknown. Once they know that others will help with the packing and sorting, and that they have a chance to look at possible alternatives, it might be easier for them to contemplate a move.

Their home is often the family home, and offspring may find themselves unexpectedly attached to it and to its many memories. Clearing the house has a hidden emotional aspect, a form of grieving, which can drain a carer's energies and affect family relationships. The fringe benefit here is that the house clearance can be done as part of a positive move, while the inhabitants are still alive. It can be helpful to separate the emotions due to losing the family home from the pain of losing either parent, and practically there will be less sorting out of personal possessions to do later on.

Dealing with the differing needs of a frail couple can get quite complicated, and a perfect, new compromise may be hard to find. On the other hand, moving a couple together does mean that each has the support and familiar presence of the other in their new setting.

David's widowed Mum saw the need for change and had firm views about where she should settle:

> After my father died, my mother needed emotional support in her grief. Then, eight months or so after his death, she fell and broke her ankle. After coming out of hospital, she was at home

with full-time agency carers. I then lived three hours' drive away and did not see her very often. It was obvious that she would never drive again. Living in a small village with hardly any shops, she clearly needed to move.

I arranged for her to go into a nursing home, an arrangement she was very happy with, as she was disabled, fed up with having carers in her home, and burdened by a 'love-hate' relationship with the house, as it held too many memories of my father. She didn't want to live with us either, fearing to upset our good relationship with her. She settled well into the home, which is a very good (though expensive) one.

When the opportunity arose for our family to move much nearer to her, we took it. We now live only forty-five minutes' drive from her, and I can see her much more often.

Planning towards a move

The timing of a move is tricky, and there may be no ideal time to do it. However, forward planning can pay rich dividends. A carer can quietly research the options without fear of unsettling anybody, and then have a few good ideas ready to share at the right moment.

There are, as we've seen, two paths to a move: a pre-emptive strike, i.e. moving before things go wrong, or moving after trouble hits. Each has its pros and cons. Moving in a period of stability gives time and space to discuss what to do with treasured possessions, and possibly a wider range of living options. It also gives the family a chance to organize time off for the busy 'pack, clear, sell, move and settle in' period.

Moving after illness or bereavement is another path. It makes for a stressful period, with fewer options, but at least you all know what you are up against. Also, there's no danger that the elderly person is moved prematurely into

care. Moving within a few months of losing a partner is often
a bad idea, but a frail, old person may not have any choice if
their spouse was also their main carer.

For some families, as for Mhairi's, the decision about a
move is taken out of their hands:

> My mother lived in her own home until major surgery marked a
> very definite decline. She hit a crisis and was admitted to hospital
> and then to residential care – another stressful stage for us all.
> The one good thing was that we didn't need to persuade her to
> leave her house. That decision was made for us.
>
> It was a three-and-a-half-hour drive to the home, on top of a
> week at work. She wanted to come away with me every time,
> and looked so wistful as she waved us off. Very painful that was.
>
> We retired and moved to a house close by, thinking she would
> be able to live with us for a while, and she did actually have one
> or two holidays with us. But her decline meant that permanent
> residence with us was not feasible. However, she moved to a
> more suitable residential home nearer us, and now I can visit
> much more easily. The fretting about going back to her own
> home has gone. She has a greater peace now than she has had
> for a very long time.

As both Mhairi and Shenaz have discovered, sometimes
what starts as a short-term crisis-care solution can become
a permanent feature, making forward planning difficult.
It is impossible to prearrange for every possibility, which
is nerve-racking for control freaks like me. Still, it's worth
having a shot at looking forward so that there is some kind of
flexible plan in place, particularly with regard to finance, and
safe, accessible living space.

Talking it through

Moving in together, if it's an option, needs to be considered carefully by everybody in your household, including the younger generation. Once you have definitely offered to have your parent in your home, it's very difficult to backtrack. Of course your parent will also need to think and talk through how such a move might work out. You might want to try moving them in for a trial period, while keeping their own accommodation intact and setting up an opt-out clause for either side at the end of the month.

Remember to plan ahead – for example, to think about what would happen if Dad couldn't manage your stairs or get into the bath later on. Would you need to carry out renovations to the house? Is there someone who could stay with him if he couldn't be left alone all day? What services are available in your area? Allowing for decline now may help to avoid another disruptive move later on.

Look at the way you live, too, and how much you feel able to share your space. Could Dad have his own TV in a separate room? What about holidays? Will he cope with teenage music? Try to be realistic about personality clashes and other commitments at this point. Heroism can turn to martyrdom, and nobody wants to live with a martyr.

You'll also need to look at where to live as an extended family: your home, their home, build a bit on, or both move and start out in a new place? Now is the time to research, think, pray and talk honestly about living expenses, inheritance tax, and funding the shared family home, should parents go into care later on.

You may not be the only one thinking this one through. Other adult family members will have their own views and plans. An offer of weekend or holiday respite care could make all the difference to your life as a live-in carer, or perhaps Mum would prefer to live with your sister instead of you.

I don't think we can manage

If living together looks like a bad idea, it's not just a case of home care versus care home. There's a range of options to look at, which is more than Timothy's church members ever got back in New Testament times. It might help to think about seasons of care, rather than once-for-all decisions. If you feel too overwhelmed to make decisions, make sure you are handling your emotions effectively by rereading Chapter 6.

Here's a range of ideas to start you off, and as usual, sharing the care is the way to go.

Supported at home

Your old folks might decide to stay on in their own home. They could have increased support from you, and maybe pay for other care, or get state-funded help. Remember that most home-care solutions are cheaper than residential care. A granny flat is another possibility: semi-detached living, with you close by for any need or crisis. Perhaps they would like the social aspects of sheltered housing, ideally with a nursing home nearby if it's Mum plus Dad. Then if one goes into the nursing home, the other can easily visit. You might have a short stay with them, or them with you, following a hospital visit, and when they are better, go home again. Of course family finance and state funding for care comes into the picture, and professional advice here can avoid costly mistakes.

Moving an elderly parent many miles to live near (or with) a son or daughter needs careful thought. It will take them away from their own friends, their trusted doctor and their well-known neighbourhood. If they lack the energy or health to find new friends and pursuits, they may feel lost, or dependent on just one or two busy relatives for everything. Depression is quite common in the elderly after a move to an unfamiliar place.

Of course some parents divorce and end up living in different places, or perhaps your spouse's parents are far away from your own, leaving you wondering literally which way to turn. I know a couple who gathered their three surviving parents from various places to live close to them, but not together. Other extended families make a master plan, where those who are able take on responsibility for particular elderly relatives so that the burden is spread out.

Some extended families split the year into chunks and care for their parents on a seasonal basis, moving them every few months to another household. Like every solution, this one has a possible downside: it doesn't suit every old person to be moved so often. It may prove hard for them to integrate into different communities, and find friends and interests outside the family, leaving them isolated and very dependent. Healthcare is also interrupted, which may be an issue. Extrovert types, meanwhile, may thrive on the change of scene.

I heard once about a group of seven unrelated, elderly friends living in a large city, who moved in together and had a care visit plus communal meal provided each day of the week by their different families. How's that for creativity? All the same, it must have needed a lot of planning.

The caring household

If you are doing live-in care at home, remember that you are entitled to ask for a carer's assessment to see if you qualify for help, such as money for you or practical help with your parent in order to give you time off. If it's all getting too much for you, then consider respite care, which gives you a week or a weekend off every so often. Look at local care facilities and see which one might be suitable later (the social work department can advise on respite funding and keeps a list of local care facilities), and take Mum to a suitable long-term place for her respite care if possible. Then if she needs to go in full-time later on, the staff and setting will be familiar to her.

You can ask your doctor, the social work department or the Citizens Advice Bureau what else is available in your area for home support, or go private with an agency if your budget allows. Your parent may be eligible for home care even though she lives in your home.

Some services are aimed at any old, frail person at home, but others are more focused. For example, if your parent has cancer, specialist nurses can come in to help. These nurses also provide support and information for the carers on hand, drawing on their long experience and training. This kind of free service makes home-care for terminal illness a viable option.[3]

A day hospital place offers you a break while Mum gets a professional assessment, a change of scene, a cooked meal and the chance to meet new people. Needs which emerge through formal assessment have a better chance of being met once they are on record. The way in to this system is through the doctor or community nurse. Voluntary or state-funded lunch clubs are another possibility, and may offer entertainment and outings too.

A confused or shy parent may not wish to tackle new places and new faces, but may be happier in her own familiar space with a volunteer or paid carer keeping her company while you enjoy a few hours off.

Residential care

Admission to residential care is not inevitable for an old person. It's not even all that common. Around one in five people over seventy-five live in communal-care settings; the others live in the community till their death, perhaps with a brief, final hospital or hospice stay.[4] A decent care or nursing home is a good option for those who have major care, security or nursing needs that cannot be met by the family or friends on hand. I'm talking about issues such as night wandering, confusion, continence or mobility needs. Some frail, elderly people may be better served by geriatric or psycho-geriatric inpatient hospital care, depending on their particular needs. Local doctors will know what's available and what's good, and it's wise also to ask families who have relatives in local care homes.

The Care Commission, or its regional equivalent, inspects every UK care home and offers reports, for anyone to view. You can also get a copy of the UK National Care Standards so that you can see what your parent is entitled to while living in residential care.

There are different ways to use a care home. It's a care tool, not a prison sentence. For example, in my friend's nursing home there was a room that lay empty through the weekend but was occupied during the week. The elderly woman who lived there had a son who wanted to care for her but couldn't manage through the working week, so he had her home at weekends. I knew another son who found a care home close to his workplace so that he could often pop in after work, just to say hello and check that Mum was OK. For others, a daily visit would quickly become a needless burden.

Care homes and old people's homes tend to offer less specialist care than nursing homes, particularly for confused or aggressive residents who will need more attention. For example, some homes specifically exclude dementia care. While you're at the research stage, it's important to find out what's on offer, and if the management ever ask residents to leave and why. It would be difficult all round to be forced to move Dad from one home to another when he's so frail, or add confusion to an already confused dementia sufferer.

Since the better homes usually have waiting lists, forward planning is very useful. Moving into the home can usually be deferred if Dad's not ready when he gets to the top of the list, which means he's not committed by adding his name now.

However good and pleasant a care facility is, it will always have one drawback: it is simply not like home. There will always be change and other drawbacks to face, so looking for perfection is clearly pointless. If you decide as a family that residential care is the best option, you can still honour and bless your parents. You are not ceasing to care. You are looking to care for them in another setting. Believe me, you will have plenty of opportunities to look after them there.

The care ideas below assume that you are close enough to visit regularly. If you live further away, some of these ideas will still work, and there are more ideas for your situation in Chapter 10.

Caring alongside residential care
Ahead of time
Choosing a care facility
- Research suitably placed care homes or nursing homes.
- Do the paperwork for funding, obtaining legal or other advice.
- Make an initial visit and ask lots of questions. Try popping in unannounced to ask for an appointment to

visit, thus seeing how you are greeted and how things look (and smell) on a normal day.

- Take Dad along for a second visit and let him ask his questions.
- Take time to talk through his views and concerns.
- Get Dad on the waiting list.
- Find out if he can keep his own GP. If not, look into the available options so that the changeover can be smooth.

Handling his home

- Arrange to pack up, clear and sell the house if necessary.
- Get his mail redirected – perhaps to you if he is confused.
- Raid his address book and give his new address to all his friends.

Dealing with possessions

- Get the dentist to mark his false teeth.
- Make sure he has supplies of medication to start him off, and include a note for nursing staff of when they will run out.
- Help him pick out favourite bits and bobs to have with him in the care home.
- Organize some personal / family photos with the names written on the back, and make a photo album with a little history written in, or perhaps do him a memory box. This gives the staff a sense of the whole person and him something to talk about with visitors if he hasn't much news to share.
- Buy machine-washable clothes, such as jumpers and slippers.
- Mark *all* his possessions: clothing, underwear, shoes, glasses, ornaments and pictures. Even if Dad can keep

track of his things, another patient may wander off with them, and the laundry system needs labelled clothing.[5]

Once he is in the care home
Early days

- Make sure everybody knows immediately about allergies, night wandering or other potential emergencies.
- Give him extra time and reassurance while he settles in.
- Get to know staff and tell them useful things, such as how he likes his tea and why he has that rash round his middle. This will help them to care for the whole person and ease his transition.
- Learn the routine of the care home. Find out about any extra activities he might enjoy (or hate) and tell the staff.

Keeping track

- Keep the funding side straight and up to date.
- Keep buying suitable clothes and toiletries, and check for lost or worn-out clothing
- Find his teeth / cardigan / slippers that have gone walkabout.
- Keep him in books, sweets, tobacco or other treats. Does the local library offer a delivery service to the home?

Building your team

- Thank the staff so that they feel motivated to do even better.
- Bring or send little gifts – this applies to staff as well as parents.
- Take up problems with staff on his behalf (but don't overdo it – the staff need space to breathe!).

Keeping in touch
- Visit, phone to ask after him, or speak to him on the phone directly.
- Celebrate birthdays with him.[6]
- Keep him up to date with family news and photos.
- Bring the latest baby in, or borrow one for the afternoon.
- Bring the dog in (which usually leads to kidnap by other residents).

Moral support
- Take him out to the park or café, using a spare wheelchair if need be.
- Take him home or away for the weekend.
- Hug him regularly.
- Tell him jokes.
- Take time to listen to him.
- Pray for and with him.
- Sit with him when he is poorly.
- Say 'hello' to others who have no visitors at all – now there's a new avenue of service all by itself.

I'm listing lots of ideas to show that there are many ways to continue caring and honouring, regardless of the setting.

The big move

Opting for residential care is never an easy choice to make. However, for some families the pressure of home caring is so great that relationships break down and everybody is miserable. Once Mum goes into a nursing home, her daughter gets to sleep at night (whew), and the family can visit, take Mum out and enjoy her company again. Mum meanwhile has a hoist to get her into a proper bath at last, new people to meet, and her own loved ones propping her up. Or perhaps she will take longer to settle, and express resentment towards the family for a while. Some parents need time to learn that the care-home staff, rather than their familiar relatives, will help them with daily needs. The carers too have a transition to handle and need to learn to let go a bit.

There is often no choice about nursing-home or hospital care if Dad has complicated care needs, his carer falls ill, or the situation has just got beyond what his family can offer him at home. However it comes about, admission and settling in are likely to be busy and emotionally draining for an elderly person and their family.

Mhairi remembers:

> When my Mum was first admitted to hospital and then to residential care, I felt as though she had been wrested away from me, that I had lost her. However, living in her own home she often looked unkempt. Now that she is in care, she is helped to look her best, including having her hair done weekly and sometimes even her nails! It is a delight to see her looking so bonny.

Feeling guilty and unsettled is normal during the transition to care, so if you've done your best to make a wise and loving decision, try not to revisit it endlessly. Choices and changes in old age are rarely stress-free or without some drawbacks, but even a rocky start may lead to a good quality of life once Dad has had time to settle in properly.

Whatever happens, there is no need to feel you are

Whatever happens, there is no need to feel you are required by a frowning God to do every single thing yourself required by a frowning God to do every single thing your-self. You're a parent-carer, not a martyr at the stake. It's the heart attitude that counts. If the main carer gets ill, the whole thing breaks down, so it's important to look after yourself. This means finding responsible ways to have some time off and enjoying it without guilt, however you are caring at present.

To ponder

1. Are your parents in need of more care at present? What is lacking in their current situation?

2. Looking again at 1 Timothy 5, what is the heart attitude expected of believers towards their families? Does having this attitude mean that today's believer should:
    a) do all that's needed in person?
    b) oversee it all, trying to make sure it all happens?
    c) intervene only if there is a crisis?
    d) consider it his only obligation to pay tax which will fund the State to do it?

3. Do you know the available options for supported living in your area? Is it time to do some research into the next step?

4. Have you asked your brothers, sisters, spouse, children or other family members how they feel about home-care or other care choices for your parents?

5. What do you think about the concept of caring for your parent in a care home? Do you have other ideas to add to the lists above?

'When I said, "My foot is slipping," your love, O LORD, supported me. When anxiety was great within me, your consolation brought joy to my soul.' Psalm 94:18–19

'Thought before action, if there is time.' Regimental motto

'In a hospital they throw you out into the street before you
are half cured, but in a nursing home they don't let you
out till you are dead.' George Bernard Shaw

'Trust in the LORD with all your heart and lean not on your
own understanding; in all your ways acknowledge him,
and he will make your paths straight.' Proverbs 3:5–6

'Where there's a will, there's a relative.' Anon

9. Oh, but I've tried: Sharing the gospel with elderly parents

There are two big questions for Christians considering issues of faith in their parents. First of all, what can be done to help unsaved parents find faith before it is too late? This is a loaded question for many sons and daughters, who may already be feeling like dreadful failures as the years go by and nothing changes. Next, how can a carer help a frail parent who needs spiritual nourishment at this demanding time of life?

Offering life

Starting with the question of salvation, here's a true story:

> Marion was poorly with cancer, and her son, Phil, arranged to move her in with him and his family after she broke her leg. They rearranged their small flat and four children, and Phil's wife, Denise, was happy to put her nursing skills to use while Phil was at work.

As Marion settled into her son's loving home, her resistant attitude to eternal things started to change. She was a self-sufficient person but, as time went on, she felt comfortable with Phil and Denise praying with her. This was a new development after years of patient, sensitive and apparently fruitless witness.

Denise worked from home as a childminder, and the father of one of her charges was John, a local minister. John met Marion each day when he was picking up his toddler, and they got acquainted. The two hit it off, and over the course of several weeks became quite friendly. Then Marion moved to a hospice for respite care, where John worked as chaplain.

Marion, aware of her poor life expectancy, and influenced by the love shown her in her son's home, started asking John about heaven and the Christian faith. She opened up to him in a way that she had never done with her own relatives. John answered sensitively, and helped her to understand the basics of the faith. Some weeks later, Marion had an obvious change of heart, although characteristically she didn't discuss what had happened. Her praying family were greatly encouraged as her peacefulness increased, although her body grew frailer. She died soon after that, and John preached joyfully at her funeral.

I watched this story unfold some years ago and found it a great learning experience. Sometimes we are too quick to write off any suggestion that our own parents might wish to rethink spiritual things. This situation was helped by John, who took time and trouble with a stranger. It can be very difficult to know what to do next in sharing your faith with a parent, and Marion clearly preferred to talk about spiritual things with someone outside the family. John was an answer to prayer.

Ministering acceptance

A Christian carer may long for parents to know the comforting presence of God in their latter years, and to be assured
of their eternal destiny as time grows short. However, as
we move into a caring role with parents, the balance of
power shifts. A captive audience needs to be treated with
respect, however urgent we feel about the need for salvation:
'Fathers, do not embitter your children, or they will become
discouraged' (Colossians 3:21). This verse refers to dependent children who cannot escape the leadership, company
and comments of their parents. Now the boot is on the
other foot: we need to work out how to honour our unsaved
parents and respect their right to make their own choices,
while sensitively presenting and living out the gospel. Frail,
elderly people, struggling to maintain self-esteem in the face
of loss, may be sensitive to any hint of rejection over their
long-held ideas and beliefs. On the other hand, love and
acceptance build a solid foundation for change and growth.
Mhairi writes:

> I would say that Mum is someone whose understanding of God
> was severely affected by a family situation, and she spent a lot of
> time thinking and reading, trying to get to the bottom of it. She
> was from an era when faith was 'a private thing'. So anything
> approaching 'witnessing' to her made her very uncomfortable.
> I pray that the Lord has entered through the 'secret stairway to
> her soul'.

What would Jesus do?

In Mark 10:17, Jesus meets a rich young man asking about
eternal life. Jesus listens carefully to him and asks questions
to help them both understand the situation. He looks at

this man with genuine love (verse 21), and speaks the truth
to him. Once Jesus addresses the root of the issue, the man
withdraws in sadness, because he is not ready for radical
change. In verses 22–23 Jesus lets the man go without blame,
argument or compromise.

Jesus cared for this young man and wanted him to enter
his kingdom. He knew what the man needed to do, and
answered his questions plainly. What he didn't do was force
or manipulate him to change. Jesus welcomed people with
love, met their needs and told them the truth in the power of
the Holy Spirit, as his Father had sent him to do. This is how
he opened the way for them to be saved according to God's
purpose.

Jesus was not defensive when dealing with angry or
misled people, because he knew who he was: the light of
the world and the Son of God. He understood his role in
bringing change: 'No-one can come to me unless the Father
who sent me draws him . . .' (John 6:44a). Jesus taught freely,
not withholding the message he had come to bring. He had
confidence because he knew his Father's words had mighty
power to change hearts and open blind eyes. However, love
always opens the door to pain, and for Jesus it was indeed
painful to see his message ignored: 'As he approached
Jerusalem and saw the city, he wept over it and said, "If you,
even you, had only known on this day what would bring you
peace . . . you did not recognise the time of God's coming to
you"' (Luke 19:41–42, 44).

If we are to serve successfully, as Jesus served, we need to
understand that lovingly speaking words of life is different
from forcing change upon others, and that love opens us up
to the pain of rejection as well as the joy of seeing new birth.

What can I do now?

Many Christians have shared their faith with their parents for decades without apparent success, and consequently feel a sense of despair or defeat. What remains when sensitive witness is rebuffed? Here's a six-point plan.

1. **'Live a life of love' (Ephesians 5:2)**
   In this season of life we have many opportunities to show our parents that we really love them, and to display the work of the Holy Spirit in our imperfect lives.

2. **Rest on the truth**
   Who is responsible for a conversion? The Holy Spirit's role is to convict of sin, reveal the truth, and carry out other wonderful transactions that we will never understand. This leaves the Christian to live a Christ-like life, to pray for the person, and sensitively and helpfully to present the claims of the gospel at a suitable time. Our role is enough for us without trying to expand it: we certainly can't respond for another, far less take the place of God.

3. **Share the load**
   We can be like Phil, Denise and John above. Is there someone suitable who is willing lovingly to befriend and encourage your parent?

4. **Share your faith creatively**
   Dementia, deafness or other progressive disability may make it difficult to communicate the basics, never mind abstract ideas. As always, our carers have different strategies. Mhairi has found new ways to reach out to her Mum, who has a church background:

   She is not capable of understanding any line of discussion on spiritual things now, but I find it easy to say things like, 'I heard

OH, BUT I'VE TRIED 149

your favourite hymn on *Songs of Praise*', and then sing it, praying
that the truths will reach her spirit. Or when driving around with
the hills ahead of us, I say, 'I to the hills will lift mine eyes . . .',
and she will finish it with, '. . . my help cometh from the Lord.'
It's interesting how things learned way back in childhood still
remain.

5. **Serve in prayer**
   Whatever your situation, prayer is always possible.
   Bringing your parent regularly into God's presence in
   prayer is an amazing way to serve them. Pray for guidance too about how best to serve in bringing your parent
   closer to God, and ask God for good friends for him/her.
6. **Resist condemnation**
   Guilt, condemnation and worry over the eternal future
   of your parent lock up your ability to pray effectively for,
   relate to or share with them as opportunities arise. It's
   worth praying regularly to be free from such negative
   emotions. It's neither 'spiritual' nor helpful to be locked
   into guilt and gloom.

Fostering faith in old age

So how can a carer encourage a Christian parent in their
faith? It must be taxing and discouraging to grow old and
frail, with pain and incapacity quietly increasing, and some of
the old ways of finding strength now out of reach. Some old
people can't get to church meetings now, for example, and
at times that also includes the hard-pressed carer who can't
leave Mum or Dad.

Shenaz says:

Up until a fortnight ago, my mother came to church with
us every Sunday, but it became clear that she was finding it

increasingly difficult to get into the car. She didn't like the loud music, fell asleep and snored during the sermon, wanted to leave immediately after her coffee, and generally complained. We tried a taxi there and back, but she didn't want to wait for it to come! Now she goes to day care on a Sunday, so that we can still go to church with the kids.

Finding new paths

If church attendance is out of reach, spiritual needs don't disappear, so a new way of communing with God is needed. It's helpful to ask your parent how they most easily connect with God, if that's possible, and try to work creatively to help them continue to enjoy God's presence.

Reading the Bible can become difficult, so a large-print or audio version may be needed.[1] A parent may enjoy praying with their carer, or perhaps a prayer meeting could meet around the parent once in a while instead of in an inaccessible upstairs hall.

Familiar Christian music is encouraging, if hearing allows, and can be played at home or through earphones with an MP3 player in a nursing home or hospital. Earphones are also handy at home if Mum needs the volume up too high for others nearby. Christian radio and well-chosen online sermons can also bring encouragement. Some churches have whole services available to view online.

A minister or another pastoral person could visit, offering an isolated parent the chance to speak to someone other than the family about faith or other personal matters. Inviting a Christian friend for a visit could also help to give fellowship and encouragement.

If Dad really enjoys nature as a setting for meditation but can't go for long walks as he used to do, how about a plant to care for, a natural history programme to watch, or a drive in the nearby countryside? Even time sitting in the garden may help to refresh him.

For those who connect with God while doing acts of Christian service, inactivity hits hard. Could you set up a link between Mum and the local youth worker, missionary abroad or other suitable person or group, with updates, prayer pointers, and perhaps the opportunity to give money towards a specific project? This works both ways, supporting the person doing the work and giving Mum a real sense of purpose.

If it's time to choose a care home for a Christian parent, is there any spiritual input available? Once he is in residence, he may not get out much, so a well-run service on the spot will make a real difference. If Dad's own minister is far away, a designated chaplain will mean that pastoral visits are easily available. The book In a Strange Land[2] includes a special short service to be used at the time of admittance to a nursing home.

Believers with dementia may worry that they may forget their faith or even forget God. This frightening prospect can be gently countered with solid truth: whatever happens, God will not forget us.

Here's how Julie supports her mother in her faith:

Mum is a Christian and takes an interest in her church, reading the monthly denominational magazine. She can't go to church services now because of her agoraphobia, but we go to coffee mornings and suchlike. She reads and discusses her magazine and takes an interest in her family's church life also.

Her faith is very important to her, and I know she prays a lot, especially for family members. She likes her daily Bible readings, and sometimes she'll talk to me about what she has read. She listens to the service on the radio at times, and also the Sunday evening service. We share what we pray about in the family.

(If your parent is of another faith, you can respectfully adapt the six-point plan, while arranging pastoral visits from the rabbi or whoever.)

Bring your needs to God

The Gospels show that Jesus took a genuine interest in the sick or needy and those who cared for them, often rearranging his day to make time to help them: 'When Jesus came into Peter's house, he saw Peter's mother-in-law lying in bed with a fever. He touched her hand and the fever left her, and she got up and began to wait on him' (Matthew 8:14–15). Jesus was Peter's friend. They spent a lot of time together, planning, praying and ministering to others. So it was natural for Peter to ask Jesus to come home for a meal. When they arrived, Peter's mother-in-law was sick, so Jesus healed her. The close relationship between the two men had spilled over into blessing for Peter's family.

Other Gospel stories show the loving friends and carers of sick people asking Jesus to come to their aid, imploring him to heal from a distance, or physically bringing their sick to him.[3] These carers knew that only he could make things change.

Their actions and requests were the same as our prayers today, for we too have a trusting relationship with Jesus, and direct access to his ear day by day. Our God truly takes an interest in our parents' present and future well-being, and our own. This means that prayer can be the carer's powerful secret weapon.

To ponder

1. Do you find it easy to discuss your faith with your parents?

2. Do you feel guilty about your parents' spiritual state? Take time to pray and shake off condemnation. Then ask God how to be a blessing to them this week.

3. What barriers might your parents face in expressing or building up their faith?

4. Have you seen answers to prayer in your caring work?

'It is the duty of every Christian to be Christ to his neighbour.' Martin Luther

'To disagree is one thing; to be disagreeable is another.' Anon

'A little faith will bring your soul to heaven, but a lot of faith will bring heaven to your soul.' Martin Luther King Jnr

10. But I'm so far away! Honouring from afar

Many extended families find themselves scattered, perhaps living a hundred miles apart or on opposite sides of the world. This means that, when elderly parents hit a crisis, there may be nobody on the spot to help. Other families have one relative or more at hand, with others at a distance, and so each one makes a different contribution to the team effort, something that brings its own pressures and resentments.

Faraway offspring tend to feel guilty, worried and helpless as parents age. They often feel powerless as they hear of growing needs and difficulties, and they worry over what is happening without their knowledge. They may spend hours trying to resolve issues created by distance, such as trying tactfully to keep an eye on someone who is unseen. The nature of parent-care tends to be a series of small, daily supportive tasks, and this is very difficult to achieve for a distant carer. The inner soundtrack runs: 'What can I do? . . . I feel so useless . . . I should be there, but I need to be here.'

Visits are often quite intense, as having come all that way means staying for days or weeks rather than enjoying an afternoon together. It can feel like feast or fast, together or far apart, with neither situation totally satisfying. The day-to-day changes in an ageing parent break painfully upon a visiting son or daughter. They can find themselves sucked into the politics of who does what, or may disagree with the tack taken by other helpers. Parents or siblings may not appreciate the reasons why visitors live so far away, which brings additional pressure to bear.

Many distant carers feel they are not caring at all because they are so far away. They simply do not realize how hard they are working to help their parents, or how they themselves are being affected by the situation.

A time to serve

In fact there are plenty of useful things a faraway carer can do. Here are some ideas to start you off. If you are in this situation, you probably have your own strategies to add.

- Pray regularly for your parents.
- Show up when they are ill, moving house or at any other key time that they need extra support.
- Phone or write regularly, so they feel up to date with your news. An adjustable phone helps a deaf parent to enjoy a phone call.[1] Phone to remind a forgetful parent to keep an appointment, or to ask how it went.
- Pay for helpers, or support volunteers in other ways.
- Support their local carers in any way you can. This improves their morale, which then impacts on your parents day by day.
- Do a respite week or weekend for your parents to allow other carers to have a break.

- Take your parents away for a day or two, or bring them back to your house for a change of scene.
- Send personal photos, cartoons or newspaper cuttings which you think they will enjoy. Ring parents up to share a joke.
- Look on the Internet for suitable clothes or household goods, or to track down and arrange local services for your parents.
- Send thoughtful birthday gifts.
- Send flowers or other treats, or a greetings card, just to say hello.
- Cook meals for the freezer when you are visiting, for them to enjoy when you are gone.

It's easy, and paralysing, to feel that nothing will be enough. Yet here's the truth: nothing is too small to offer to someone you love, because it speaks so loudly of your love and interest. You can do small things, believing in a big God. However you choose to serve though, try to avoid doing or suggesting anything that would make more work for the hard-pressed carers on the spot.

The power of encouragement

Everybody has heard of the master painter Vincent van Gogh. Have you ever heard of his brother Theo? Yet, without Theo's help, Vincent would have given up long before painting his finest works. Theo's letters to Vincent have been preserved, and they show how Theo constantly reassured Vincent of his great talent, comforted him when things went wrong and often sent money for the rent, or for paints and brushes. Theo himself was not artistic and never achieved personal greatness, yet his kind encouragement made Vincent's creativity blossom despite his mental frailty.

Here's what the Bible says: 'Encourage one another daily' (Hebrews 3:13a). We often overlook or miss opportunities to encourage others, but it's a scriptural command, and we know it feels wonderful to be on the other end. The simple gift of positive truth has mighty power to improve another's perspective, or to put courage back into them. We have opportunities every day to minister encouragement to one another, and so encourage ourselves along the way.

Whoever is looking after Mum or Dad today is in need of your encouragement, be it your sister, your other parent, step-parent, neighbour, home help or the care-home staff. Don't let diffidence stop you from saying a few kind words in the right place. It may feel like a small thing to write a short note, to ring and ask how things are going, or to say 'well done', but it can make a huge difference. In fact, your frail parents themselves will walk taller after a dose of encouragement from you, even if you are far away. Words of encouragement and a listening ear hold serious power.

Jan reflects:

> For my mother, the primary carer is my sister Nancy, who herself has multiple sclerosis and a son at home with Down's syndrome. How she copes with it all I don't know. I don't think it works fine for her at all. I am 500 miles away, but Nancy is phoning increasingly often to talk about it all, so I am happy to be there for her.

Absent-saint syndrome
Another aspect of faraway caring can have interesting results. The carer on the spot, serving away day in day out, can find she is put in the shade when another relative turns up. For some reason, elderly parents often overlook, or complain

about, daily service rendered, while endlessly talking about the visitor as if they were a saint, complete with halo. This is hurtful and irritating, and can drive a wedge between sisters and brothers in no time at all. A quiet chat behind a parent's back can knock out the wedge, but altering the parent's approach may not prove quite so easy.

The absent saint is well placed to broach difficult subjects while she is visiting, for example, to lobby for unpopular but necessary changes, or to point out the front-line carer's needs. She may also take other liberties, such as spring-cleaning or throwing things out. This shares the pressure with the carer on the spot, and it's amazing what a fresh face can get away with!

It can be tricky if the visitor chooses to do things differently, and it's usually better to respect the strategies of the front-line carer who is doing the job all year round.

Visits can be hard work. Here is Jan again, holding the fort while her sister has a much-needed break:

> I sometimes go and see my Mum, staying with her in her home. I cook meals, do shopping and washing (clothes, not her), and escort her to medical appointments. This happens while Nancy is unavailable so, for the duration of my trip, I am the front-line carer. I feel 'at work' all the time. I make a point of going out every afternoon to get away, and bringing shopping back with me.
>
> The hardest aspect is to be with Mum all the time. I can't even read a postcard on her mantelpiece, for she interrupts everything I try to do, like watching the TV, reading the paper – everything – but she expects to be uninterrupted while doing those things.
>
> I am always glad to come home again!

A short but useful visit

The Bible is a bit quiet about faraway parent-caring, which is probably because most people lived out their lives in their home villages, so the elderly were usually cared for by the family, on the spot. However, Exodus 18 describes a few days which Moses spent with his visiting father-in-law, Jethro. Moses had probably lived and worked close to his wife's family during his forty years in Midian, but had been too busy for family concerns during the exodus. Jethro still lived in Midian, and Moses was then camping in the desert area of Rephidim, around 300 miles away, so it was quite a trip for an old man to make.

Although leading the nation and frantically busy at the time, Moses made time to meet Jethro as soon as he arrived. He greeted him respectfully and warmly, and the two spent time together catching up. Jethro watched Moses at work for a day, worshipped with him, met all his friends, and finally gave pointed advice to his son-in-law, who was chasing his tail ruling all those Israelites.

If I had been Moses, I might have thought, 'Interfering in-laws, just what I need. What does he know about leading a nation? He's not even the right religion. Doesn't he know I am a national hero and no longer just one of the boys?'

Moses, of course, was wiser than me. He listened respectfully to Jethro, thought it over and decided to take his wise advice in verse 24. This saved Moses' health and made the system of government sustainable. Moses heaved a sigh of relief, junior leadership began training for the future, and the whole nation was greatly helped. Jethro went home feeling welcome, significant, useful and loved – a pretty good outcome for a weekend visit, eh?

To ponder

1. How far away are your parents? Is distance a problem to you?

2. Is there someone looking out for your parents who might appreciate a bit of encouragement? Write a note of thanks and post it today, or send an email. It doesn't need to be long.

3. Does absent-saint syndrome ring a bell with you? Do you need to discuss this with certain people to make sure you are in a good relationship with them?

4. Why do you think Jethro's visit went so well?

'Distance is just a test to see how far love can travel.' Anon
'Without God, nothing is significant. With him, nothing is insignificant.' Anon
'Law of the bath: when the body is fully immersed in water, the phone will ring.' Anon
'Nobody can do everything, but everybody can do something.' Anon

11. Freed by the truth: Dealing confidently with decline and death

Parent-carers naturally deal with a less healthy season of life, often faced with a lot of parental illness, including life-threatening crises. We may feel at times that we have no hope of rising to the demands of our workload, however much we love our parents. Carers dealing with an increasingly complicated situation can lose confidence and long to withdraw. A carer whose parent has many medical problems can feel overwhelmed by the level of home-care required of them. Another stress factor is the level of supervision required to ensure that everything happens properly, on top of all the other tasks.

There's another difficulty lurking here. Despite the best possible care, our parents will decline over time, before finally dying and leaving us behind. Some carers may be so scared to face this change that we try to turn back time by our own efforts, or we might ignore the whole issue and hope it will go away. Both strategies are based on fear and denial, which drain away energy and confidence. We need a sound foundation in order to face the challenge of continuing to care through the seasons of decline and death.

God's eternal perspective

Happily, God has provided a rock-solid truth to help us as we care for someone in their final years. God's ruling responsibility is to set each person's lifespan, and our response is to care, as and when we are needed.

Here is Job talking to God about the natural order of life and death: 'Man's days are determined; you have decreed the number of his months and have set limits he cannot exceed' (Job 14:5). Job has grasped that it is God who knows and sets each person's lifespan. This is a firm reminder to those of us who keep trying to fix everything and everybody. We are not called to rescue the world from its troubles, however impressive and worthy that may seem.

Jesus highlights this concept of God's responsibility for lifespan and our response. He applies it to the area of worry: 'Who of you by worrying can add a single hour to his life?' (Matthew 6:27). He makes it so clear that it's useless and stressful to try to control things that are not our business. With respect, I'd like to apply this principle further by adding a phrase: 'Who of you by worrying can add a single hour to his life, *or his parent's life?'*

In the light of this truth, I'd like to invite you to relax into the beautiful words of W. C. Smith's famous hymn, based on Isaiah 40:6–8:

> We blossom and flourish as leaves on the tree,
> And wither and perish; but naught [nothing] changeth thee.

God is the one who is immortal, not us. He is the one who will never leave us, or change his wonderful nature. We can rely on him in a changing world.

Get real
A friend and I were chatting recently about the challenge of finding confidence to care for frail parents. She wisely compared parent-care to a beach trip in our famously uncertain Scottish weather, an idea that grabbed me immediately. So roll up your towel and come along with me . . .

Scene one: Normal alert
There we sit on the beach, blue sky, toes in the sand, tartan rug and sandwiches unpacked, children pottering blissfully with plastic buckets. It's so peaceful. As I lazily turn my head, I spot black clouds gathering on the horizon with surprising speed and determination.

Scene two: High alert
Keeping an eye on those clouds, we prepare the troops to bundle everything into the rug and run for it. For the moment though, we picnic on, knowing that any minute now we'll have to finish off, perhaps wetly. But it's still fun; in fact maybe it's even more fun knowing that it's all going to end soon.

I find this illustration very helpful in shifting my focus from the future, which I cannot foresee or control, to today with its challenges and satisfactions. Every passing day brings possibilities for an old person and their carer, and a successful moment, hour or day is not spoilt by subsequent troubles.

These are simple everyday principles: living for the day, accepting what we cannot change, letting God be God and giving our daily service in his world. Yet these principles have a lot to do with delivering satisfying, relevant care to our frail parents, even in uncertain times. Let's see where the pitfalls of unreality might lie in wait for parent-carers.

Death.com

Part of our trouble lies with our culture. The processes of ageing, decline and death are carefully concealed from us these days, and giving birth is rapidly going the same way. A professional approach to the whole business is now the norm, when it used to be a family affair. It's no wonder that we don't always grasp that death is part of life. Many of us have never been at a deathbed or even seen a laid-out corpse in his Sunday suit. Our elders are often tucked away in care homes, sick people whizzed off in ambulances, and death managed by undertakers (in a closed coffin, please), as soon as the last breath is taken. No wonder we find ourselves out of our depth by a deathbed, or when Dad can't manage to make it to the shops any more. We have lost our traditional skills.

We have lost the knack of relaxing into God's timing

Another problem for some Christians is that we have lost the knack of relaxing into God's timing. We see every new challenge or difficulty as something we need to put right, maybe by repenting, or praying against it. Although it is important to seek God and pray over difficulties, it also helps to remember the principle of being content in all things and then looking to see God's purpose in them. This can transform our anxious perspective – how do I make it stop? – into a confident, expectant one – how will my Father work for good in this?

What we can (and can't) do

If we aren't able to save our parents' lives by worry or sheer hard work, what use are we to them as they go through the process of decline and eventual death? Well, we can't solve every problem, but we can learn, listen, love, do small things well, and bring comfort in the hardest of times. As we serve and care for our parents, we learn to know them better, and a deeper love can grow.

I enjoy this insight from the life of Job. In remembering the happy days of his prime, Job lists the ways he served his community, including his ministry to the dying and bereaved: 'The man who was dying blessed me; I made the widow's heart sing' (Job 29:13). We too can pray to be anointed with this ministry, to be a comfort and support to the dying and the bereaved. I'm not suggesting that it's easy to watch well-loved parents decline, but rather that we can find a positive, useful role for ourselves at a difficult time.

We are not invincible

Carers cannot afford to ignore their own health, however hairy things may be at home. Back problems and stress are very common but can easily be prevented or lessened. The occupational therapist can teach you how to lift your parent safely, and stress relief needs to be a priority along with all the others. Yes, it's hard to make time, but a sick carer means a completely stranded parent, often at no notice at all, as Elisabeth discovered when she suffered a nervous break-down due to overwork. How did this affect her approach to her responsibilities?

> I suffered a period of complete memory loss, and was then admitted to a psychiatric hospital for several weeks. This was partly due to the stress of caring for my parents. This has had a

big impact on me. I have had to take serious stock of my lifestyle, admit I'm not twenty-two, learn more about saying 'no', try to relax, trust God more, and accept help from wherever it is offered, and even seek help when I see warning signs of overload.

The expert carer

Any carer can benefit from support and training to manage their job properly. The hands-on home carer is the obvious example of this, but there are other possibilities too. A parent in a busy hospital, hospice or nursing home will also benefit from an informed relative acting as their advocate. This can be done at a distance, by phone if need be, or during a visit.

Carers can learn about illnesses and treatments from other carers, the Internet, the local library, their bookshop, or by asking the doctor or other professionals. Perhaps there is a carer course available. Try the local or national association catering for your parent's condition. Many have helplines where you can talk issues through or find information. A carer who learns on the job gains confidence and is better equipped to continue.

Mhairi found that being her mother's advocate was vital when her mother moved:

Liaison with my mother's professional home-care team, and keeping track of who was going in when, from a distance, was quite a feat, but I felt secure and supported. Then, when Mum was admitted to hospital, there was a whole new set of personnel to try to get to know. It was incredibly difficult to connect with constantly changing staff. They did not know her, and I had to develop quite a persistent approach to get the core issue addressed. I felt I was struggling through a thicket for several weeks.

This had still not been resolved by the time she was deemed 'better enough' to be admitted to residential care. More new personnel! One of these, mercifully, really listened to me one day and understood exactly what I was talking about. Action was taken and Mum quickly improved.

Getting the most from medical care

After five years at medical school, I can say with confidence that mind-reading was not on the curriculum. What a busy doctor loves is a patient or carer who gets to the point and tells all the facts. Then the doctor (or whoever) can deal with the full picture. There is no time to play games or drag out information slowly, and since a problem is what the patient has come to discuss, it's not a crime to get on with it.

In fact, sweet-faced denial is a waste of a consultation for all present. A list of issues can be prepared by the parent and carer ahead of time and given to the doctor on arrival ('This is what has been happening/has changed since . . .'), or read out during the consultation. This saves time, cuts through denial and makes for helpful clarity. Lists are also a good way to organize important questions beforehand so that they don't get forgotten in the heat of the moment. It might be useful to take notes on what's said and decided, particularly if the situation is so stressful that details might be forgotten.

But I don't want to be a bother

A problem arises when a parent is in denial, or can't see how their health has changed. They may object to a carer 'telling on them' or be too embarrassed to discuss personal topics such as continence. Some elderly people have a feeling that they shouldn't bother the doctor, and will smile and deny pain or other symptoms. Later they will complain about these same symptoms to their frazzled carer, who now feels like throttling them. (See page 83, for a respectful way around this common difficulty.)

You are probably the world expert on your particular Mum, and you can work alongside the other experts to make a good life for her, but for best results, information has to flow in all directions. You can tell them about new problems, or the response to a new pill, and they can answer your questions about managing things at home.

Keeping track

As a parent's health deteriorates, life can get quite complicated. You may be the liaison person for a wide range of services and people, and things can easily get overlooked. A lot of carers end up chasing up their rights or their parent's rights at some point. Taking notes, keeping track of correspondence and phone calls, and asking questions as you go along will help you remember who promised what. Getting it in writing is also a good idea at this stage.

A calendar, wall chart or notice board for your parents' affairs is a must, and saving letters, phone numbers and appointment cards in a designated spot helps too. The calendar can also be used to look back on and keep a note of who has visited, particularly if Mum has memory problems. Asking people to ring you, not your deaf or confused mum, to make appointments *for her* can save many a muddle. Pills can be sorted once a week into a divided box marked with times and days of the week, so that your parent (or her helper) can see whether or not she has missed a dose.[1]

Your ill parent is likely to end up with a key worker, such as a family doctor or social worker, whose job it is to coordinate the care team. A sympathetic, well-informed key worker is a great asset, but you may still need to check things yourself.

Unexpected blessings

Those who care for very ill parents can find good things along the way. Most carers learn on the job, and most elderly people decline over time, so the complicated stuff comes bit by bit, not all at once. Even with a gravely ill parent, caring tasks, particularly those involving touch, can be a two-way source of comfort and a powerful bonding experience. There can be a sense of pride and job satisfaction as the carer gains new skills for the sake of love. Another hidden advantage is the sense of personal growth, of rising to the challenge, and seeing God's provision.

Elisabeth admits:

> I have no previous experience of care for the elderly and very little of social services, including funding issues. I have frequently felt out of my depth! As time has gone on, I have understood much more that seemingly insoluble situations actually give opportunities for new levels of trust in a faithful God, who hears and responds to cries for help. I never thought I would say it, but I value this opportunity to see how much bigger God is than I had previously experienced.

When a parent is dying
God's timetable

Psalm 139 celebrates God's creative role in human life. King David rejoices because God knows us as individuals, and has made us personally and with care. God knows the end from the beginning, and he loves us throughout our lives, come what may.

For you created my inmost being;

    you knit me together in my mother's womb.

I praise you because I am fearfully and wonderfully made;

    your works are wonderful,

    I know that full well.

My frame was not hidden from you

    when I was made in the secret place.

When I was woven together in the depths of the earth,

    your eyes saw my unformed body.

All the days ordained for me

    were written in your book

    before one of them came to be.

How precious to me are your thoughts, oh God!

    How vast is the number of them!

(Psalm 139:13–17)

This beautiful psalm helps us with two big issues in terminal care: personal worth and the ending of life.

According to King David, each person is known to God and precious to him. The value of a human being is not just in their failing abilities, sick mind or ageing body, but in their unique spirit, which will never die. Their last days or weeks are as important as the rest of their lives, because each human individual retains significance throughout their life.

We may wonder why a very sick person has to struggle along when hope of recovery has gone. The philosophy behind euthanasia takes this several steps further, and claims that a sick person (or their attendant) has the right to choose their time to die. Verse 16 puts this issue beyond doubt. It's God's place, and his alone, to number the days of a life.

On the heels of this truth comes verse 17, describing the peace and security of following a God who thinks often of us. We are not alone, declares King David, and our loving Father is fully in charge.[2]

Time to talk

As a parent nears the end of life, they may have things on their minds that they wish to talk through. They might want to be open with family members about the fact that they are dying. Perhaps they are afraid of what lies ahead and want to talk about this honestly, without being jollied out of it. They might want to talk about practical matters, such as a will, the disposal of their belongings or the future care of a surviving spouse. They might want to discuss the afterlife too, or to reflect on past events.

It may be scary to contemplate discussing death with your parent, yet the alternative is to leave them alone with their most troubling thoughts. You don't need to know all the answers to be a supportive listening ear. A simple offer may release Mum or Dad to talk things over. Following their lead in conversation frees you from the worry of straying into areas that they are not ready to discuss.

We have seen that Christians are not free to pre-empt their own time of death, or to help another to die, but this doesn't leave families powerless at the end of life. There are other important choices to be made and carried out, such as considering and planning for home, hospice or hospital care, organizing a will, deciding who the parent wants to see, and all the small, daily personal choices that uphold our dignity. Some people want to make a living will, stipulating any medical intervention that they wish to avoid in their last days or weeks.[3] If such issues are not considered, the only alternative is to take whatever comes, which may not be for the best.

From your own point of view, bereavement is unavoidable and so too are the emotions that follow. However, there are things to do now in order to avoid painful regrets when it's too late. If there are important things to say or ask, hugs to hug, and thanks to be offered, why wait? Too many people find themselves at the funeral, sadly wishing they had expressed love and gratitude, or sorted out a grievance. There is no need to wait until death is near to say your piece, and of course we need to remember that some people die without warning. You can do this kind of sharing without the impetus of terminal illness, and it may be easier to do it when life is going well.

If there are important things to say or ask, hugs to hug, and thanks to be offered, why wait?

If you find it difficult to talk about personal things with your parent, perhaps you could write a letter that expresses how you feel. They may be openly pleased or possibly reserved but, whether they comment or not, you have had the chance to say what matters to you before it's too late.

Coping with terminal care

Many people fear the process of death because they don't know what to expect. A chat with the doctor, nurse or other health professional can improve your confidence. It is not unloving or morbid to ask about the probable lifespan of a parent and, if you are near the end of your tether, it helps to have some idea of how much more care will be needed. Perhaps home-care nurses could help bear the burden in those busy last days, or other relatives or friends could come along and pitch in.

If your very ill parent has to move from home into another care setting, please don't let feelings of guilt spoil the closeness of these last days or weeks. It's not a failure on your part to go for the most suitable care. Your parent will still find your familiar company reassuring. If you want to continue doing some of the caring, do ask. Busy nursing staff are usually pleased to have help.

The end of life

As a doctor, I have been present at many deaths, the vast majority of which were peaceful, with a sense of God's presence. God is not frightened of death and can be relied upon to stay close to us, just as he is faithful in other seasons of life.

For the dying believer and his carers there is an added promise: 'Precious in the sight of the LORD is the death of his saints' (Psalm 116:15). The word 'precious' here implies 'carefully watched over'. Death may seem like the ultimate, terrifying loss of control to us, but the Almighty God is close by.

An expected death

Elisabeth and her Dad knew that death was approaching. She shares this honest account:

> Dad's last days in the nursing home were agonizing. Advanced Parkinson's, cancer, arthritis and angina rendered him immobile, in pain and with no appetite for food or any activity. He was unchanged 'in there', and the last thing he managed to say was a prayer of thanksgiving. He continued to be appreciative after speech was gone, something I could see in his eyes. A few hours before he died, he was struggling to get his arm out from under his duvet. I lifted it out and gently placed it on top of the covers. The slow response of a 'thumbs up' said it all. That was his last communication.
>
> Dad had wanted to go home to heaven for a long time, and several times we had prayed together, expecting it to be the last

time, because he was sure he was dying. The relief when Dad
died, quietly, peacefully, just forty-five minutes after I had left
him for the night, was enormous. The loss had been happening
over months and, to know he was home, safe, whole and
fulfilled, was wonderful. I never cease to be grateful for the peace
and expectancy we have because of the certainty of heaven.

An unexpected death
Sudden death brings different challenges for a carer. There is
no warning to get ready for major upheaval and loss. Mike
lost his Mum during the writing of this book, and looks back
over her death and its aftermath a few months later:

> It was stressful caring for Mum at home as she got worse,
> especially the last two weeks when I was facing the fact that
> it was all too much for me. I knew she wouldn't understand
> this. I had excellent paid carers in the mornings to get her
> up, but otherwise, as an only child, I was unable to share the
> responsibility with anyone. I was not aware that these were her
> last days.
>
> On Friday she ate well, read most of the day and had a short
> walk in the garden. She went to bed a little early. I went down on
> Saturday morning to find her unconscious on the floor. I called
> the ambulance, went with her to hospital and kept vigil through
> the day. I went home at 9pm, and she slipped away during the
> night without regaining consciousness. I had no time to think or
> prepare.
>
> Reflecting on my time as a carer, I recognized it was my duty.
> There was no-one else to do it. Mother wanted to be at home to
> the last, and I am so glad I was able to fulfil that wish. I believe
> God took her at the right time, and I am at peace that I could not
> have done more. She had a good, long and fulfilled life.

Maybe it is still too early to assess the impact of caring on my life. Taking on less work may have meant less income. Certainly some ministry opportunities were lost, and it's difficult now to get back into the swing of things. Perhaps I do feel I've lost a year or more of my life.

Grief and change

Bereavement is a big deal. This book is not the place to tackle the aftermath of losing a parent, but it's worth remembering that a carer has redundancy to add to their other losses. However much a carer may long for release from caring work, it is something familiar, giving structure to the day. On the other hand, natural relief over the end of a parent's suffering and the end of heavy caring responsibility also feed into a carer's grief. This makes for a complicated mix, with the usual emotions of bereavement, such as shock, sorrow, guilt, anger and disbelief. As the journey of grief begins, it can help to know that the person who has died was well looked after.

Often there are other mourning relatives to support, perhaps including the surviving spouse, who may also be frail or ill. This is a very intense time for any family, and there are no easy answers out there. Time must pass and emotions must flow before recovery can begin.

'Even though I walk through the valley of the shadow of death, I will fear no evil, for you are with me' (Psalm 23:4). This familiar verse encourages those who mourn to work through their pain and look to the future. We do not endure the grief process for ever, although it often feels as if there is no way out at the time. We have God's firm promise of protection and company as we walk through the valley and out into the next phase of life.

Keeping company with the saints

I was paying a visit one day to close friends who fostered children. In the friendly noise and clutter of their playroom, little Aneako asked me for a Bible story. I took her on my knee and asked if she had a favourite one. Her foster-mum smiled and handed me the Bible with a bookmark already in 1 Samuel 2. 'Aneako always wants the same story,' she said, 'the story of Samuel growing up in the temple and his Mum making him a bigger robe each year.'

I thought this was an odd choice for a five-year-old, and began to tell the story before the significance hit me and I ground to a halt. Aneako had recently been rescued from a life of neglect and abuse, arriving scared, filthy and famished, clinging desperately to her younger sister. In this new and unfamiliar setting, she had connected to Samuel as a person like her, a young child who had been fostered. This was important business. I began again, really trying to tell that story, and explain the meaning in a way that would give her hope.

As I look back, I see that Aneako had discovered a secret that many others also appreciate. We look in the Bible for characters and stories that relate to our own lives. Reading their stories, we feel less alone, and we can learn about the way God has lovingly dealt with people like us in the past. This is a lifelong treasure store for us all.

So who might we choose to keep us company as we care for the elderly? We could do with seeing love and faithfulness in action, but we must also confront bleaker themes such as loss, decline, helplessness, grieving and dying. We need biblical companions who will stick around when the going gets really tough.

Faithful friends in a crisis

Matthew 27 tells the stark story of the crucifixion. Christians naturally tend to focus on the crucified Jesus, but there are other riches here for us too. As the Lord hangs suffering on the cross, where are his friends? 'Many women were there, watching from a distance. They had followed Jesus from Galilee to care for his needs' (Matthew 27:55). We know from John 19:26 that John, the disciple 'whom Jesus loved', was also there with them. He had run away earlier with the other disciples, yet had come back quietly to share the vigil.

How did these people feel? They had travelled with Jesus for many months, and truly loved and trusted him. On top of the shattering blow of his arrest, now they were watching him struggle for breath, taunted by passers-by and bleeding from brutal wounds. They had failed to grasp that this was part of God's plan, so they had no sense of future meaning to comfort them. They must have longed to rescue him, or even to wipe his bloodstained face, but they had to stay at a distance. Yet they refused to abandon him, although they could do nothing for him, and he could do nothing for them.

Dr Sheila Cassidy, torture survivor and hospice director, comments that waiting at the foot of the cross is the hardest, yet most important, aspect of caring for the suffering. Active caring is much easier for us to cope with. We say, 'If only there was something I could *do!*'

The power of being present

When we ourselves suffer, we long for a solution, but we know that other things help too, such as companionship, love, respect and acceptance. These things seem too small and powerless to offer when faced with decline and death, but let's read on and find out how such service was rewarded. In Matthew 27:61 we leave two devastated women sitting by the grave, all hope ended. In 28:1–8 we find them watching the resurrection, right before their eyes. The surprising joy of Easter Sunday was uniquely theirs, simply because they chose to be there. In verse 9 they meet the risen Christ himself, shining brightly, pain wiped away for ever. Their vigil was completed as they knelt to worship him and then received his instructions.

This passage teaches us the high value that God places on standing at the foot of the cross, even when we would rather be miles away, meeting our own needs, or just hiding from our helplessness. It's good to know we are not the only ones to pass this way.

To ponder

1. Do you find yourself expected to do things for your parent that you've never done before? How do you tackle this?

2. Have you had any training in caring, or in your parent's particular health problems? Try to make time this week to research what's available locally, or to find some information that you can read at home.

3. Do you have things you would like to say to, or ask, your parent some time? Make a note and try to do this soon.

4. Would you agree that being present with a suffering person makes a difference? What barriers do you feel are most difficult in serving your parent in this way? What attributes or skills do you have that might be useful in this setting?

'Nursing is an art: and if it is to be made an art, it requires an exclusive devotion, as hard a preparation, as any painter's or sculptor's work; for what is the having to do with dead canvas or dead marble, compared with having to do with the living body, the temple of God's Spirit? It is one of the Fine Arts: I had almost said, the finest of Fine Arts.' Florence Nightingale

'There are no great things, only small things with great love.' Mother Teresa

'Some people think that doctors and nurses can put scrambled eggs back into the shell.' Dorothy Canfield Fisher

'I've learned that, regardless of your relationship with your parents, you'll miss them when they're gone from your life.' Maya Angelou

'I will not leave you as orphans; I will come to you.' John 14:18

Afterword

Elisabeth reflects:

God has set us in families for a purpose: caring for one another through the various stages in life is the outworking of his encouragement to 'love one another', and to care for the weak.

My views on parent-care have changed – perhaps matured. For a long time I didn't actively consider that God might have a view. What I did, I did because I loved my parents, and because my support was needed.

Some months ago, a friend was asking how things were going, given the complexity of caring for relatives who lived widely apart, and having had to lay aside other ministry to do this. She said simply, 'Caring for widows and the vulnerable is close to God's heart.' That brought it to the top of my consciousness, and of course I had known it deep down, but I found it very helpful.

To be able consciously to share the caring with God for this

season, knowing that clearly it's an expression of his love and
plans, brings real joy and appreciation of this period in the midst
of the emotional pressure.

As we finish, it's time to reflect, along with Elisabeth, on
the way we tackle the job of honouring our parents. Here
once again is the parent-carer's commandment, the gold
standard as we care for and celebrate our frail parents:
'Honour your father and your mother, so that you may
live long in the land the LORD your God is giving you'
(Exodus 20:12).

We've seen that living in God's ways is only possible as
we are joined to him in intimate relationship. The DIY alternative is stressful and ultimately fruitless; instead, we are
called to live confidently as beloved branches of Jesus, our
true Vine, with his power and grace flowing out through
us. Living in God's provision gives a firm basis to our work
as carers, and sets us free to respond to this commandment
without fear.

As we seek to build strong relationships within our
churches and communities, it is my prayer that the unmet
needs of parent-carers will be seen and met. In this way,
we can be drawn closer together in love and learn to serve
others. This is a foundational part of God's plan – for us
to live in loving relationship with him and with others
around us.

In the centre of God's will

It is encouraging to know that parent-caring is not in the
small print of God's Word, even if sermons about it are thin
on the ground. It is right up there in the Ten Commandments
and emphasized throughout the Old and New Testaments.
This is truly a central part of our Christian commitment, so

we can confidently expect God's presence and provision as we work.

The word 'honour' means recognizing merit or distinction, showing special recognition and respect, looking up to or deferring to a superior person, or showing reverence. As carers, we're honouring Mum or Dad as people, then honouring what they have done for us in the past, as well as honouring their life-giving relationship to us. The Hebrew root of the word 'honour' used in Exodus 20 translates as 'to weigh heavily', so our parents' concerns are to be important to us.

Of course, honouring is not always the same as pleasing or appeasing. It's about showing healthy respect, consideration, practical service and love. It's the exact opposite of neglect, calling for us to be lovingly involved with our parents in whatever way we can.

Like many carers, David looks back to the love and care he received as a child:

> I think about all that my mother did for me when I was a child, so I am only repaying a great debt of care that was long ago offered to me. It's a privilege to be able to help when you are needed. It's quite a responsibility as well to be needed like that. I'm grateful that mine is not as demanding as many other people's experiences of caring for elderly relatives. I'm glad to be able to make a real difference.

God with us

The second half of the commandment contains a promise concerning the rest of the carer's life: '. . . so that you may live long in the land the LORD your God is giving you' (Exodus 20:12).

As we have seen, carers need to find ways to care for themselves too, and the church should be playing its part in helping wherever possible. This promise has power as we cooperate with God, share our lives and responsibilities with others, and make time to care for our own bodies, which are after all temples of the Holy Spirit.

The promise has a broad sweep, which is encouraging when caring responsibilities seem to shrink life down to four walls. God oversees our lives and knows that one day the season of parent-care will naturally come to an end. He is actively planning and doing good things for and through us, and training and equipping us for those future times, as we honour our frail parents now.

To ponder

1. Has your view of parent-caring changed as you have read this book?

2. Do you feel there is too much on your shoulders at present? How could you work towards sharing the load?

3. Do you have regrets about any aspect of your caring work? If so, take some time to pray and lay this burden down at the foot of the cross. No need to lug it any further!

4. Do you know a parent-carer you could encourage? Is there a way your church could support parent-carers or elderly people?

APPENDIX

Here's a selection of resources and information for the more common situations faced by parent-carers. If you know of other useful books, helplines or resources, please contact Emily by emailing comment@emilyackerman.co.uk. Emily also invites you to visit her website at www.emilyackerman. co.uk.

Books

Jean Clayton, *The Tiny Red Bathing Suit of Mr. July: Inspiration and Resources for Continuing Care Providers* (Wood Lake Books, 1997) – a hospital chaplain looks at the experience of old age and assisted living.

Neil Coxon, *Dear Grandad, From You to Me: Journal of a Lifetime* (from you to me ltd, 2007) – other titles available: gift books with questions about an older person's life and memories, for them to fill in and give back to the younger generation. See also www.caringmemories.net, below.

Malcolm Goldsmith, *In a Strange Land: People with Dementia and the Local Church* (4M Publications, 2004) – an excellent Christian book on dementia and dementia care.

Jackie Highe, *Now Where Did I Put My Glasses? Caring for Your Parents – A Practical and Emotional Lifeline* (Simon and Schuster, 2007).

Sharon James (ed.), *The Dawn of Heaven Breaks: Anticipating Eternity* (Evangelical Press, 2007) – an uplifting anthology of Christian writing and poetry about heaven, dying and faith.

Hugh Marriott, *The Selfish Pig's Guide to Caring* (Piatkus Books, 2009) – a famous, funny and useful book about caring.

Jane Matthews, *The Carer's Handbook: Essential Information and Support for All Those in a Caring Role* (How To Books, 2006) – a general book about caring.

Louise Morse, *Could It Be Dementia? Losing your Mind Doesn't Mean Losing Your Soul* (Monarch, 2008) – a practical, uplifting Christian book on dementia.

Louise Morse, *Worshipping with Dementia: Selected Scriptures and Prayers for Sufferers and Carers* (Monarch, 2010).

Louise Morse, *Dementia: Frank and Linda's Story – New Understanding, New Approaches, New Hope* (Monarch, 2010) – about a couple handling the husband's dementia.

'The Milk's in the Oven', a booklet about dementia for children and young people, published by the Mental Health Foundation (www.mentalhealth.org.uk).

Penelope Wilcock, *Learning to Let Go: The Transition into Residential Care* (Lion Hudson, 2010) – a Christian look at the transition from independent living to residential care.

John Wyatt, *Matters of Life and Death: Human Dilemmas in the Light of the Christian Faith* (IVP, revised edition 2009) – a Christian professor of ethics and perinatology reflects on medical ethics.

Online resources

www.ageuk.org.uk – the website of Age Concern, a large charity working for and with older people, which has lots of information and useful links.

www.alzheimers.org.uk – the Alzheimer's Society website has a wealth of information, including recent research findings on dementia.

www.biblesociety.org.uk – for audio Bibles and lots of other
   Bible-related resources.

www.carecommission.com (tel. 0845 603 0890) – Scottish regulatory
   body with lots of information about care standards, including
   access to reports on every care home in the region. Grades 1 and
   2 are unacceptable, 3 and 4 are OK, 5 and 6 are very good.

www.carers.org – carer support and information website run by the
   Princess Royal Trust for Carers.

www.carersuk.org – an organization campaigning for carers, and
   gathering information about their needs.

www.caringmemories.net – information about making a life-story
   album.

www.chandlercaregivers.com/Docs/Caregiver Syndrome.pdf – an
   interesting account of strategies to combat caregiver's syndrome
   in the USA.

www.cinnamontrust.org.uk – a UK charity helping older people care
   for their pets. They offer dog walking and other practical help.
   The charity also provides pet foster care for when owners are in
   hospital, long-term pet care with owner visits if an owner goes
   into residential care, and continuing pet care when an owner dies.

www.cqc.org.uk – the equivalent regulatory body for care homes in
   England.

www.crosslinescotland.org – this site offers trained Christian
   support via email.

www.crossroads.org.uk – a charity that cares and campaigns for
   carers, with local groups throughout the UK. Links here to sister
   Scottish and Irish websites.

www.macmillan.org.uk – UK charity providing all kinds of advice,
   symptom control and practical support for people with cancer,
   and their carers.

www.mariecurie.org.uk – UK charity providing free terminal
   nursing care in hospices and at home (not just for cancer), plus
   information and support for family members.

www.mind.org.uk – website run by MIND, a major mental health
   charity and activist organization.
www.opsi.gov.uk – the Office of Public Sector Information, for legal
   standards of care and other government information.
www.pilgrimhomes.org.uk – runs Christian care homes for the
   elderly in England.
www.publicguardian.gov.uk – government agency handling power
   of attorney. Has downloadable forms for different regions and
   general advice about the process of DIY registration.

Websites for young carers

www.youngcarer.com – the National Young Carers Initiative, for
   child and teen carers.
www.youngcarers.net – advice and support for young carers.

Telephone support and information

Arthritis Care helpline: 0808 800 4050.
Cancer helpline: 0808 800 1234 – manned by cancer nurses, run by
   Macmillan Cancer Support.
Carers Christian Fellowship: 01793 887 068
   (www.carerschristianfellowship.org.uk) – organization offering a
   quarterly newsletter with pen-pal facility, email and phone prayer
   chain, occasional retreats and quiet days (some local groups).
Carers Helpline: 0808 808 7777 – UK government-funded helpline
   dealing with local government services and benefits.
Crossline England: 0845 33 77 789 – offers trained Christian support
   by telephone from 6pm to midnight every day.
Dementia helpline: 0808 808 3000 – run by the Alzheimer's Society.
Elder abuse helpline: 0808 808 8141 – for anyone worried that an
   older person is being harmed.
Samaritans: 08457 90 90 90 – 24-hour phone support, also email,
   face-to-face or postal support for anyone.
Stroke helpline: 0303 3033 100 – run by the Stroke Association.

NOTES

Acknowledgments
1. From 'I Hear the Sound of Rustling' by Ronnie Wilson, copyright 1979, Thankyou Music.

Chapter 1
1. If you'd like more about God's view of the elderly and vulnerable, try Leviticus 19:32; Psalm 146:8–9; Matthew 6:1–4; and Galatians 6:2.
2. All names have been changed.
3. All these parent-carers are adults, but of course there are younger carers too. There are many children and teenagers caring for disabled, ill or addicted parents, often without support. If you are one of them, I hope you will find some encouragement here, but this book is aimed mainly at adults. However, you will find information about services for young carers in the appendix.
4. In 2007, people caring informally for family or friends saved the UK government an estimated £87 billion. By contrast, the total government spend on the NHS in that year was £82 billion. Each carer saved the country an average of £15,260. (Source: L. Buckner and S. Yeandle, 'Valuing Carers' (2007). Full text available from www.scie-socialcareonline.org.uk).
5. See Ruth 4:13–22 and Matthew 1:5–16.

Chapter 3

1. Dr Jean Posner, a neuropsychologist who has studied the syndrome, defines it as 'a debilitating condition triggered by unrelieved, constant care of someone with chronic illness'. Source: P. L. Latham and J. Posner, 'Caring for Persons with Dementia' (2007), available from www.strokeassociation.org

2. You'll find more about managing embarrassment, guilt and worry in Chapter 6.

Chapter 4

1. Elisabeth's aunt and Dad died during the writing of this book, and I've included her comments just as they were written. This comment arrived before either died, so at this point she was juggling her own household plus two parents at a distance and two aunts elsewhere.

2. See the appendix for information on making a life-story album.

3. Brother Lawrence, *The Practice of the Presence of God* (Revell, 1967).

Chapter 5

1. This subject can be further explored in *Boundaries* by Dr Henry Cloud and Dr John Townsend, revised edition (Zondervan, 2002).

2. *British Medical Journal* 2005; 331:1548–1551 (24 December), available at www.bmj.com

Chapter 7

1. See the appendix for information about life-story albums.

2. G. Cohen, *The Brain in Human Aging* (Springer Publishing, 1988).

3. Jean Clayton, *Journal of Pastoral Care* (1991): see also her book in the appendix.

Chapter 8

1. You can download forms and find out more about the process from the Office of the Public Guardian website (details in the appendix).

2. Help the Aged has information on wills and Lasting Power of Attorney. Contact details are in the appendix.
3. www.macmillan.org.uk is a good starting point.
4. Source: UK Office of National Statistics.
5. Ask the nursing home beforehand how they like articles to be marked, for example, with initials, name or room number. A laundry pen inscription or woven name-tapes need to survive frequent industrial washes.
6. If your parent can't eat cake because of diabetes or eating problems, he can still enjoy hearing the happy birthday song, and perhaps blow out a candle in a holder, or watch while you blow it out.

Chapter 9
1. Try the Bible Society (see appendix for contact details).
2. See appendix for details.
3. Matthew 8:5–13; 12:22; 15:21–28; Mark 2:1–12; 7:31–37; 9:14–29; Luke 7:11–15; 8:40–42; 8:49–56; John 4:46–54; 11:1–44.

Chapter 10
1. The RNID sell adjustable phones.

Chapter 11
1. Boxes are available from your pharmacy or online from www.medimax.co.uk
2. For more on Christian medical ethics and terminal care, try Professor John Wyatt's book, *Matters of Life and Death* (details in the appendix).
3. Age Concern have a fact sheet on Advance Directives, Advance Statements and Living Wills (contact details are in the appendix). The legalities may vary in different regions of the UK.